Mike Sh

Diaries of
The Unbalanced Paddleboarder

*crash
and*
RISE

From Victim to Thriving Survivor

Life to Paper Publishing Inc.

Toronto | Miami

LIFE TO PAPER
PUBLISHING INC.

For more information and special orders, address: tabitha@lifetopaper.com

FIRST EDITION

Editor-in-Chief: Tabitha Rose, Life to Paper Publishing Inc.

Editing & Proofreading: Richard Campbell, Guided Life Stories and Brenda Rogers

Cover Design: Arash Jahani

Publisher: Life to Paper Publishing Inc.

www.lifetopaper.com

PRAISE FOR THIS BOOK

"I knew from the minute I met Mike Shoreman that he was a real-life blend of Aquaman and Superman - and this book will show any budding superhero how not only to deal with their life's big kryptonite, but also how to thrive because of it."
GIOVANNI MARSICO, Founder of Archangel

"Mike is an inspiring individual, with an amazing story."
CHRIS BERTISH, Speaker, Best Selling Author, Waterman, & Conservationist

"In Diaries of The Unbalanced Paddleboarder: Crash and RISE, Mike lays himself bare with a story of adversity, perseverance, and personal triumph that will leave you breathless. His indomitable spirit and sense of humor leaps off every page and will land right in your heart."
BRITT EAST, Author of A Gay Man's Guide to Life

"Mike Shoreman - Before, you were a great Paddleboard Instructor. Now, you're an inspiration to others and catalyst for change in their lives."
TONY HORTON, Author, creator of P90X, & Ramsay Hunt Syndrome survivor

"This is a riveting story of self-discovery and triumph. While it's personal to Mike, it's universally relatable; from strife, with the right mindset, we can all find balance again."
CODI SHEWAN, *Author of Everyday Legacy: Lessons For Living With Purpose, Right Now*

"Mike Shoreman revealed one of the most inspirational stories we've ever heard when he shared how he retrained his brain (and mind) to do what doctors said could not be done after a crippling diagnosis. His story is not only a shining example of why you must swim and not sink when the waters get rough, but how positive thinking and saying YES to your best self can completely change the tide of your life."
KRISTEN BUTLER, *CEO of Power of Positivity*

"Mike Shoreman's speeches have impacted many and we at Innerlight Media are more than happy to help share his messages to inspire more people."
TRAVIS BLAKELY, *CEO of Innerlight Media Group*

"Mike Shoremans' book, Diaries of The Unbalanced Paddle boarder: Crash and RISE is about his amazing journey through life's highs and lows and trials beyond measure. How he found his way and decided to swim rather than sink. I was inspired to read about his journey of growth and overcoming many obstacles. Mike's ability

to assess, game plan and overcome is one that will inspire thousands, it inspired me!"
BILL SCHUFFENHAUER, 3x Olympian/Silver Medalist, Team USA

"Whenever someone uses their voice to share their truth, the world heals a little bit. Human connection begins in our resonance with each other's pain, joy, and the roller coaster ride in between. When we see ourselves in someone's story it's an opportunity to envision an entirely unique outcome. What a gift! *Diaries of an Unbalanced Paddleboarder* is an endearing and heartwarming adventure following the high highs and the low lows of Mike Shoreman. I've been lucky enough this past year to have a front-row seat and a VIP pass to the Mike Shoreman Show. Resilience, brilliance, innovation at it's finest. Relationship building, community building, momentum on steroids. Heart, soul, determination and passion. And beyond all else, a thesis exploring what it really means to be seen and heard in this world. At Speaker Slam, our core mission is to be a platform to have our speakers seen and heard and have them shine in their beautiful vulnerability. Mike Shoreman is our poster child."
RINA ROVINELLI, Co-Founder of Speaker Slam

"Mike Shoreman is one of the most inspirational people I've ever met...and his book captures one of the most inspirational stories I've ever read.

Crash and RISE had me hooked from beginning to end. The rawness and authenticity of Mike in this book, as he goes through some of the biggest ups and downs in his life that anyone could imagine, had me laughing, crying, feeling deep fears and despair...and above all fired up and ready to take on the world. This book will speak to the depths of your soul and remind you that no matter how much adversity you've faced in the path...and the cards of life all seem stacked against you...you can rise above it and have an incredible life. Thank you, Mike, for being a living example that anything truly is possible when you become your own advocate, allow yourself to receive support from others, and commit with unrelenting determination to your biggest dreams."
ANDREW SARTORY, Gay Man Thriving Founder, Gay Dating and Relationship Expert

"It takes the same amount of energy to do something small as it is to do something big. And with the odds against him, Mike used his energy to do something big. Crash and Rise is a beacon of hope for those who are facing tremendous challenges in their lives."
HELEN HATZIS, Founder, Aloha Toronto & Chief Community Officer, Genius 100 Foundation

"This is BY FAR one of the most inspirational books you can read especially if you are shrouded in darkness. This book will help you see the light at the end of the tunnel. No matter what you're going through, you can find power in your pain and change the trajectory of your life. Mike's story is very relatable. This book takes you on an emotional journey. Mike's humor shines through making this book an easy read while showing the impact of life when our health goes wrong. Mike's life may not have gone according to his plans, but the way he handled it and turned his misfortune into a global movement is nothing but inspiration.

This is a MUST READ."
DAN SHAIKH, CO-FOUNDER OF SPEAKER SLAM

"An incredible story on perseverance, hope, self-discovery, and the human spirit. Like Paddle Boarding, Figure Skating is one of those sports where falling is absolutely inevitable, but it's having the drive, the will, and the ability to get back onto your feet and continue moving forward. I'm in awe of Mike's strength and inspired by his resiliency, courage, and passion. No matter what life throws at him, he always finds a way to get up and regain his balance!"
JASON BROWN, 2014 Olympic Bronze Medalist, 2015 US National Champion, 7 Time Grand Prix Medalist in the sport of Figure Skating

"Crash and Rise' will have you laughing, crying and in awe of Mike's incredible journey. It's such an amazing story of discovering oneself through trials, tribulations and self-compassion. No matter what you might be struggling with, this book will leave you feeling like anything is possible."

"Mike Shoreman deftly presents a journey that will resonate with anyone who has ever felt quagmired in their dark night of the soul. Now more than ever do we need a message of hope and perseverance."

"#PADDLESUP has become the war cry of thousands of paddle boarders all over the world after Canada's Mike Shoreman became everybody's darling by overcoming a debilitating illness with passion and determination - I knew, almost a year ago that this story would be good but a year later on, it's even better! If you want inspirational, read Crash and RISE!"

FOR MY PARENTS,

who raised me to believe that anything is possible.

"Mike Shoreman – Hey, my friend, we fight on!
Exercise was impossible for me for many
months, but now it's how I improve. It's a real
struggle some days, but I try not to judge it.
Before, you were a great Paddleboard Instructor.
Now you're an inspiration to others and catalyst
for change in their lives."

TONY HORTON is an American personal trainer,
author, and former actor. He is best known as creator of
the commercial home exercise regimen P90X. He is also
a Ramsay Hunt Syndrome survivor.

TABLE OF CONTENTS

Draw your chair up close to the edge of the precipice,

and I'll tell you a story.

F. Scott Fitzgerald

INTRODUCTION

I remember being four years old in a big city park. And as four-year-old's go I was adventurous, curious and some might say, a damn terror, as are many children at that age.

Walking along with my parents, I saw them. Ahead of me. My eyes grew big and I knew I had to get them. All of them.

My little hand broke free of my dad's big one and I charged them. Ten of them. The geese.

I ran. Screaming and yelling, laughing. I ran.

I ran fast and so did they.

Running fast, running far.

Away they went, flapping ahead of me.

Until they stopped.

You see, those ten geese figured out they had me. I was only a little guy. Party of one.

Outsmarted, outnumbered, outplayed.

There is power in numbers. There is strength in community.

They stopped and they turned their heads over the top of their long necks to stare straight at me with those beady little eyes.

My eyes got bigger and my yells switched from laughing to screams of terror.

I ran as fast as I could through the blades of grass on that hot June day right into my dad's arms.

Up and into his grasp, I was saved from the geese-in-attack mode.

In many ways, however, I kept running.

I ran, and ran, and ran.

Running.

Through life.

Through my high school years and into my twenties.

Away from my twenties, into my thirties.

I ran from relationships, and into relationships.

I ran from east coast to west coast.

From job to job. Continent to continent.

Running.

Running away from the "geese" in my life.

I ran from me before I trusted in myself. In who I was, who I am. What I could do. What I will do.

I ran and I ran fast.

Through months.

Through seasons.

Through years.

From one thing to the next.

Until I stopped running.

Until I couldn't run anymore.

Forced to stop running.

Nowhere left to run.

Forced to stop. To be still.

It's time the world stands still.

The power isn't in running.

The power is in stillness.

Stillness.

Because when you slow down, you learn. You grow and realize beautiful things about yourself, the world, and others that you were too busy running from to ever see.

You learn gratitude and you become appreciative of all things.

And you finally have time to look behind you, and you see that the geese stopped chasing you long ago.

CHAPTER ONE

The cameras were out on the water as we paddled in front of the skyline until sunset. It was beautiful and the skies were alive with pinks and purples. This was meant to be romantic because it always had been. But this time I wasn't feeling it, and I knew that our relationship was over. Yeah, we just grew apart - like boards drifting astray on the water. We both loved paddleboarding, but it wasn't the same. I knew that. It was over. The people around us and in our circle of families knew it was over before we did.

I had asked him to come to India with me. I said, "Come with me on this sequence, and let's try to work on our relationship."

The answer was no.

Then as the stars came out that evening, the city lights flared up. This was supposed to be romantic, but it wasn't. It was almost like my call to action, seeking something truly on my own for once.

When you're in love, it's the answer to everything. It's that beautiful feeling you get when you are with somebody who builds you up and lights you up. It gets you up in the morning. It drives you to do things. You look better and you feel better. Nothing is wrong when you're in love. But all of a sudden, you wake up one day and realize it's over. It's not there; you feel empty. You feel really, really empty, and then you need to find something else. But without that loss, I would never have looked. That's what drove me so deeply into self-exploration, searching through my loneliness and darkness. Ultimately, it would take me to where I am today. So, I'm grateful. I knew what I was doing, that it was reckless and scary. I took a lot of risks - with travelling and meeting new people.

"You should come with me; it'll be good for us. It will be some time away together to reconnect," I suggested to him.

I shook my head to convince myself and chugged some water as I finished saying this, already knowing the answer. And I knew I didn't mean what I was saying. Knowing though didn't protect me from the response I got, and I felt this would be one of the last times we would be together. Our boards, knocking gently, sat side by side buoying up and down as the sun began to set over the towering buildings in front of us. The night had all the elements of a perfect romantic evening, but this was far from that because I knew we were approaching our end. Our relationship had run its course and for the last year or so I had been trying to play catch up, hoping to convince us both that what we had built together was worth something, was valuable, was sacred. But the truth is that it had been years since we were swept up in romance and we each were wanting and needing different things the other was not capable of giving.

"No," he replied. "This is something you need do to for yourself."

My love of India or rather fascination with India, I should say, began with watching Julia Roberts in *Eat, Pray, Love*. It continued with *Slumdog Millionaire* and finally, while flipping channels one late night, I stumbled across a program about Indira Gandhi. I was the furthest thing from being spiritual or enlightened when I decided I had to go to India. Believe me, I would rather tell you I was, but I am going to do this right. Initially, I had planned to travel with my partner at the time. I felt that we were slowly drifting apart and I thought this trip would be a really good opportunity for us to work on our relationship. As I mentioned earlier, my partner did not want to come on the trip with me. If that wasn't the clear indicator our relationship had run its course, I don't know what was. I realized he was right. I needed to go on this trip on my own. I needed to do this for myself.

I chose India because I had this dream of swimming with elephants. I was going to ride on their backs, emerging out of the waters like an apparition. It was an image I had, one that didn't survive reality. It was just a dream and I let it go. The elephants weren't even there! The excitement built as I planned for months. Then I booked my tickets and travelled the 7,625 miles on my own. This was the biggest trip that I had ever taken by myself. I was very excited, but also very nervous. I didn't realize just how big a trip or how monumentally life-changing it would be. Off to the Andaman Islands I would go! While researching how to get there, I discovered that I was going to have to travel through India. That's why India became part of my plans.

Toronto to Dubai. Dubai to Mumbai. I am okay with flying, but I also don't enjoy it. This might sound crazy, but I do not sleep on planes because I have it in my head that if the plane is going down and I am awake, I can somehow make a bee-line for the exit and save myself. Always alert to the fact that I might have to save myself at any moment, I can be hyper-vigilant to the extreme.

On the day of my first flight, I was up at nine am and we departed at 10 that evening. We flew for 17 hours, throughout which I did not sleep a wink. Instead, I thought about what I would be leaving behind - all that I would be missing back home - especially not being able to paddleboard while on the trip. Paddleboarding had become an extra arm to me. It had become a huge part of my life and being away during the month of June, I would miss it. *In the evenings or on the weekends I would paddle out on Lake Ontario. My favourite was at sunset, watching the planes landing over me, looking at the city skyline as the sun snuck behind the buildings and the sky lit up in pinks and purples.*

I was drained by the time I landed in Mumbai. When the plane finally touched down, I collected my bags from the baggage claim, and there it was: a massive rogue cow by the baggage carousel. As I approached to get my bags, I glanced over to see it making eye contact with me, and then it took a huge crap. Immediately I was second-guessing my decision to come on this trip. *This is not me at all.* For that to be the first thing that I saw - well, it made me second guess everything. After grabbing my bags and giving the cow a disapproving look, I squeezed some hand sanitizer in my palm and raced toward the exit for some fresh air. The doors opened and the thick humid air hit me. I then jumped into one of those "rickshaw" taxis they call tuk-tuks to take me to the hostel I thought looked good in a guidebook I was skimming through seven hours earlier. I was totally unprepared, but this was what adventure is and I wanted it. Here I was, completely exhausted and full of anxiety. I needed to sleep. But of course, my adventure was only just beginning. My driver ended up getting lost and driving in circles through rural India and then urban India for what felt to me like another 17 hours.

When we finally arrived at the hostel, I was in full-on breakdown mode as the Indian sun rose, afraid of what was awaiting me behind the front door of my accommodations. I won't sugarcoat it. The situation did not look pretty. I wasn't surprised when I saw a family of cockroaches scurry across the floor as I entered. They were massive, bigger than my hand, like New York City subway rats. This was my worst nightmare. I thought to myself, "There is no way I'm going to be able to sleep here." My eyes began to water, and my throat felt like it was tightening up. I needed sleep and was horrified to think about the other options there were in the early hours. I climbed the creaky stairs to my room. With the door closing behind me, I checked under all the sheets and pillows to make sure I did not have any unwelcome visitors. Sleep-deprived, I passed out.

The next day I explored bustling Mumbai. To put it simply, it was crowded, uncomfortable, and loud. The smells of the combined pollution with whatever mystery meat was cooking were heightened by the heat. Everything was so foreign to me. After about a day of walking around Mumbai, I had enough. I realized I had to get out of there. *This just isn't working for me.* This was not *The Best Exotic Marigold Hotel* with Judi Dench. This was not *Eat, Pray, Love* with Julia Roberts. This was parades of cows walking down the street and some crazy shit that was just not okay and I needed to get out, fast! At the end of the first full day, I booked my escape by train to the next province.

Looking back, I honestly believe that I was the problem. The uncertainty of a new place different from everything I had ever experienced in my life, combined with the exhaustion and anxiety I was feeling, was not a good combination. The first place I landed was bound to make me feel disoriented. I have heard from friends who also had similar initial reactions when they landed in Delhi.

Sometimes we need to remove ourselves from our lives to evaluate and make changes within. Although I was uncomfortable at first, I had a feeling the moment I landed in India that I was on the right path. It all made sense. I was an adventurer as a child, a dreamer. You could often find me at the park or in the water. I absolutely loved climbing things. I was content alone, but I enjoyed playing with others too. This was very much how my trip would go. I travelled alone but enjoyed my time with others as well - learning about them, their stories, where they came from, and where they were going - here and in life.

The next day I hopped on a train and went down to Varkala Beach in Kerala. It was completely different from my Mumbai experience in every way possible. The home-stay I was booked into was in a cliffside village overlooking Varkala Beach. It reminded me of the Jurassic Coast in Devon,

England, *sans* dinosaurs. No velociraptors here yet! It was a two-story, whitewashed home, and every room had a private balcony with a hammock. It also had the following bonus: no cockroaches!

Finally, the trip I had prepared myself for was about to begin. As I walked the hundred-something steps down to the beach toward the ocean I could hear the waves crashing, and the smell of salt from the air hit me. Being close to the water would bring me back to a state of balance. This was my natural habitat. After all, I was a water baby. I've loved swimming ever since I was a kid. I went on to spend my days on the sand, talking to locals and people watching. My nights were for indulging in authentic Indian cuisine, like tikka masala vindaloo or fish curries.

On my third night, I decided to watch the sky while swinging in the hammock on my balcony during a crazy storm. The entire sky, as far as I could see, was full of lightning. Lightening is fascinating. Never underestimate what we can learn from a Reese Witherspoon movie. It reminded me of watching *Sweet Home Alabama* and learning about the process of how lightening turns sand into glass. You are probably really impressed with me right now, but the truth is anyone can rent that movie and learn about it.

Now, back to my story. Lying in my hammock, I could hear the waves crashing on the shore below. I wrapped myself in a light blanket to shield my body from the cool night's breeze. And then it happened. Nothing could have prepared me for what came next. Out of nowhere, a giant cockroach-like bug, bigger than my hand, flew through the night at rocket speed. I felt it smack the side of my head. *AGHH!* Of course, all of the lights in my room and around the village simultaneously went out. I found myself in complete darkness. It was not a masculine sounding scream that left me. That scream could possibly be heard from India to Toronto. I heard someone approach me. I turned around to see a stubby bodied woman dressed in vibrant colours making her way toward me. The woman who worked in guest services said, "Good sir, are you okay?"

I knew at that moment that she was my Baywatch lifeguard and I was being rescued. However, when she realized the cause of my hysteria, she began laughing uncontrollably. I burst out in shared laughter as the lights came back on. Then I saw the kindness in her eyes, and it was that which I will never forget.

Near the end of my time in Varkala Beach, I stumbled upon Rita, a friendly traveler from Lithuania with long flowing brown hair, sun-kissed skin, and an unforgettable laugh. We met at a cute German bakery that was perched on top of a cliff overlooking the turquoise ocean. When I first spotted her, she was sitting and eating at a table, alone - clearly travelling by herself. I sat at the table right next to her.

We began chatting until it dawned on us that we should just sit together. So, we did. The conversation was effortless and fun. We ended up meeting for a few other meals, talking about life, where we came from, and sharing our dreams before going off on our separate adventures. Rita was the first of many fellow travelers that I went on to forge relationships with. I set off on this trip alone but was reminded after meeting her about the importance of connection. It is in sharing our stories and our dreams that we truly get to know ourselves. At least, this has been my experience.

Staying in Varkala Beach for a few days allowed me to gather the courage to explore the rest of India. I am forever grateful for this place, without which I would not have felt comfortable to complete the remainder of my journey. The tranquility that came with being near the water and connection with others on similar paths helped me ground myself.

Never arrive in Goa during a monsoon. Goa is full of picturesque beaches that can rival anything in the Caribbean and is postcard-worthy, but when you add a torrential downpour, it takes away from the allure. It was sticky and wet. My adventures in Goa involved me exploring moss-covered ruins of burnt down Catholic churches from long ago. They stood barren, basically rubble. I could tell that I was standing in a place of history. It was still a heavily Portuguese influenced state, the remains of which were barely standing.

Being in Goa was the first time I was exposed to the unsavoury underworld of India. I saw the scammers and the drug-pushers. To my surprise, there was a lot of crime. Of course, it was Goa where I picked up a copy of *Shantaram*, a book so well known to travelers through India and as big as the Bible. Seriously that book was like a weapon. It was about a man escaping an Australian prison, fleeing to India and living in the shadows of corruption and darkness until he discovered his light. As the monsoon pushed through, I finally got to see some of the beauty of Goa. It was a shimmering landscape of white sand beaches, vibrant colours, and sultry seas.

A few weeks into my trip, I found myself eating dinner with travelers in Goa. The cafe was open concept and I could see outside to the dirt road and a herd of cows swinging their tails, making their presence known in the crowded street. We sat on the floor on top of coloured cushions with fairy lights and candles all around us. I heard beautiful, seductive Hindi music. I am pretty sure this singer made the Top Three on Indian Idol. She sounded like the Eastern version of Kelly Clarkson. I inhaled aromas of curries being made in the kitchen as we laughed, drank, and shared stories of our experiences. We told tales of our travels and where we would go next. Somewhere between my Chai tea and my vindaloo I looked out to the street and saw an old man on a bike. He was disheveled looking and wearing tatty clothes with rips in them. As I turned my head back to the conversation with the girl standing next to me, I heard it. The crash! Followed by a begging, pleading cry.

"My eggs! My eggs!"

At that moment all seven of us collectively went to him. Without signaling that we were going to do this, we all raced out to the street. And there he was, lying on the gravel road with eggshells all around him. His bike was a few feet away - the wheels still spinning. He was covered in egg yolk. A few of us ran and grabbed his bike and lifted it, while the others helped to get the man up on his feet. The Australian, the Americans, the Italians, the French guy, the girl from Ireland - we all wanted to help. Our wallets opened and we each gave him some rupees to help cover the cost of the eggs that he had lost.

A couple of days later, I found myself back at that same restaurant. I had such a lovely evening that I just wanted to revisit it one last time. This time I went by myself. Not long after I placed my food order, I saw the exact same man with the eggs from the other night. To my utter shock, like clockwork, he crashed his bike, again. As before, eggs were smashed all over the ground around him. "That bastard!" I thought to myself. This was a scheme he had thought up to take advantage of people's kindness towards a stranger in distress. I was angry. Walls went up and I felt guarded. I held on to that for a long time. I refused to eat eggs for the rest of my trip as a statement to the universe. It was some sort of protest to a higher power.

I took the train up from Goa to Delhi. And I liked Delhi, but I used it more like a hub for my day trips. Indian trains are something everyone should experience at least once. They are completely out of this world. Even deciding what class to sit in is more complex than applying for a marriage license. First, you have to decide if you want a seat, or if you want to sit on the floor, or if you want to sit on the roof, if you want air conditioning or not, if you want food or not, what kind of food; the list goes on. So many options. It's fantastic and the people watching is beyond anything I've ever come across.

I went for a walk one evening in Delhi. Construction workers were digging in the streets. These very skinny guys were placing brick after brick in their baskets until they were full, placing them on their heads and then carrying them metres away and returning to do the same thing over and over again.

On my first night in Delhi, I was out exploring the main bazaar and trying to decide which meat vendor was the safest. I was determined not to spend the next week in the bathroom recovering from *Delhi Belly* so I would go and stand off to the side and watch how they prepared the food, if the line was busy, and how they were sanitizing their cooking utensils. What is impressive is that you are reading the words of someone who never got ill while travelling through India.

I stepped off the train in Agra just past 5:30 am. I'm not going to lie to you. Agra isn't a very nice city. There's the Taj Mahal and that's basically it. It's not a cute village with quaint cafes, shops, and bookstores like I found in the other cities. I used a Trip Advisor guidebook to locate a restaurant with a view of the Taj Mahal. It happened to be on the rooftop terrace of a hotel. The view was perfect, and I was able to watch the sunrise over the Taj Mahal while dining on a very western breakfast including pancakes, toast, and hash browns. In a peaceful protest to the universe, I was still not eating eggs. What I didn't realize or prepare myself for was that this was going to be the hottest day of my stay. It was 48 degrees Celsius. One of the most iconic photos ever taken at the Taj Mahal was Princess Diana's visit in the 1990s. It had been many years since that happened, and I decided it was time for a new iconic photo. I wore my most fabulous outfit that day, which certainly wasn't my lightest. I thought that there would be air conditioning. It wasn't long before I was dripping in sweat. It was so humid that people were passing out on the lawns inside the grounds.

This was the first time I have ever experienced any sort of fame. It was fantastic and uncomfortable all at once. I had asked a lovely couple if they would mind taking "the photo" and the next thing I knew, about twenty people raced over and jumped into it with me. "Matthew McConaughey, we come in your picture."

That evening when I returned to Delhi, I remember feeling relieved because for the first time I was staying in a guest house with a television in my room. And they even had a few English channels! I stumbled upon *The Big Bang Theory*, of which I was never really a fan. But I actually cheered out loud in excitement. I was stoked for some entertainment from the Western world. Later that night I went to an Indian McDonald's which was definitely an experience. I had a McPaneer sandwich. No beef on the menu there!

Next, I went to Manali which is in the lower Himalayan mountains. The overnight bus ride saved me from the knowledge that this could be the end. I didn't realize before boarding the bus that I would be travelling up the mountain on very narrow unpaved roads shared by oncoming traffic. The road safety signs were hilarious. "Overtaker Beware, Undertaker is Near." When I finally arrived safely, I googled if busses had ever fallen off the cliff roads with no guard rails, and it turned out, of course, they had. Also, why look this up when you needed to go back down the same way?

I made quick friends with a few girls travelling together from Israel. They were part of the Israeli military and had just been relieved from duty. I learned from them that

Manali was some sort of mecca, a place to go for those who have been released from the Israeli army. It offered these soldiers a place to decompress and relax. Manali is a mix of India and Tibet hidden up in the mountains. We hiked and explored, and I was reminded, looking out, that this was a lot like the view of the scenic Canadian wilderness.

CHAPTER TWO

It was the beginning of a dream.

I visited the city of Varanasi for a couple of days. The first thing I did after checking in was to wander down to the Ganges river. At the edge of the river, a bunch of kids were jumping off a bull trying to have a relaxing soak. They didn't care and he didn't seem to mind either. It was nice to see life in a place known for …death. Varanasi is one of the holiest places in India where people come to say goodbye to their loved ones and lay them to rest. They first cremate the bodies and then place them in the Ganges River. They believe that this process releases the souls of those deceased from the ongoing cycle of death and rebirth. From the moment I arrived, I found it to be very spiritual and connected. I remember looking down at the river and seeing big fires surrounded by family members embracing one another and crying together. The women were wearing saris in a variety of toned down muted colours.

The vibe changed as the sun went down. It wasn't out of control crazy, but the scene was alive and full of people. There were food vendors, kids running around and playing on the shore, and groups of people enjoying the company of those around them. Street vendors brought their trollies filled with kids' toys and food to sell. The sky was painted with stars and the warm breeze reminded me that I was fully alive.

By the shore I watched as women wearing necklaces made of flower petals would remove them and place them in the water to float away. It was a tradition from another culture that completely changed my life forever. People one by one would take a lotus flower, light a tea light candle and position it in the middle of the flower, then put it in the water to float away. It wasn't long before there were hundreds of fiery flowers floating along the river lighting it up. As I was watching this, I realized I wanted to do this at home, to create something beautiful that people wouldn't forget. I could create an experience by doing this with paddleboards and turn my hobby, my passion, into a career. I saw the beautiful lotus flowers lighting up the water and thought to myself, "I want to light up the water." It was a beautiful thing to see all these people coming together in such a positive and peaceful place. And I just sat there for hours in complete amazement watching other people send these beautiful fiery lotus flowers onto the river.

The last leg of my trip came right after Varanasi. The Andamans. Most people know the Andamans as the place where the boxing day tsunami of 2004 hit. I flew from the southwestern city of Chennai to the Indian Ocean where I then got on a boat and carried on another two hours to the islands. On arrival, I was greeted by rickshaw drivers all trying to get my attention. "Beckham, Beckham, you come with me." I hopped into a tuk-tuk and told my driver to take me anywhere, "Surprise me," and he led me to a little piece of paradise. I was about to enter a bamboo hut when the next door swung open, and, well there she was, laughing and still beautiful - Rita from a few weeks ago. It was like something from a movie. The beach was behind me, with pearly white sand and the bluest water I could ever have imagined. The warmth of the air surrounded me like a hug.

Although I didn't feel alone during my trip, seeing Rita again overwhelmed me with a sense of safety and calm. I have heard this often happens to people visiting India; they will meet someone at one part of their trip and then randomly come across them weeks later in a different part of the country. I believe this is because travelers, specifically backpackers, generally travel the same routes, upping their chances of running into each other again, coming full circle. Together we spent our nights drinking warm Indian beer on the porch of her cabin and talking about life. We were avoiding snakes on the road together, and I was avoiding scorpions in my shower alone. For the first time, I shared my experience in Varanasi and my plans to light up the water when I got home.

I felt that I grew so much as a person during my time in India. It seemed like each city I travelled to, I learned something new about myself. It was such an incredible experience that I advise everyone to try it at some point in their life.

Finally, my trip came to an end. On my flight back to Toronto I looked down at my breakfast tray staring at me to see the typical American breakfast cuisine - scrambled eggs. The reality of heading home sank in. There would be no more dosas and dips in the morning. I began to think back to the man with the eggs and to digest the con to which I had fallen victim. My perspective having shifted, I now understood, this wasn't just a con for him. It was his job, his way of supporting himself and his family. He was poor. That was his reality. Instead of sitting at home and only seeing roadblocks, he found opportunity. This was a man who needed to provide for himself and his family. He was taking charge of his life and his challenges. I picked up my fork with a piece of egg and brought it to my mouth. My protest to the universe was over.

Arriving home, I found out within days that one of my sisters had declared to the world that she was in love and that she's a lesbian. Fantastic. This couldn't come at a better time. Maybe this would soften the blow that I was about to abandon all my post-secondary schooling and become a professional paddleboarder! Oh, and if you haven't already guessed, the relationship ended shortly after my return as well. It was a reminder that nothing stays the same forever.

CHAPTER THREE

My news was well-received considering that my parents work in the legal world. It's not like going to your family and saying, "I'm going to become an accountant or a journalist." I might as well have said, "I'm becoming an actor." But they wanted me to be happy and I have to say I think they were impressed with all the charts and graphs I had prepared for them.

It was now time to get certified to become an official paddleboard coach with Paddle Canada. I spent most of my free time that summer on the water training, practicing, determined to go into the certification course the strongest I could be. Morning, afternoon, and night, I was on the water.

The leaves started changing and September arrived. It was time to get certified so I could turn this hobby into a full-time career. I asked my dad to join me as a roadie to the next province six hours away: Quebec.

"I've got to go do this thing. Do you want to come with me?" I asked him. I will say that I did bill this as a great father-son bonding experience that would be highly beneficial for our relationship. He said, "Of course." My dad is always up for a little adventure. See, not everyone refuses to go on trips with me when I say it'll be good for our relationship.

He has led an interesting life, my dad. He emigrated to Canada from the U.K. in the early 1980s and ended up having me and staying. He's funny and kind. In his younger days, he looked a lot like Richard Gere. Now, he resembles Robert DeNiro in *Meet the Fockers*, but with a British accent. He's less mafia-like now and does a great impression of every *Downton Abbey* character in a single monologue. I knew this was going to be fun.

The car ride was pleasant - a little dad and son banter. We argued for almost an hour over who had control of the music, but he won the battle and we listened to *Tracy Chapman and The Wild Strawberries* as we made our way down the road towards paddleboarding, beer, and French pastries. We caught up on each other's daily lives, our future plans, and of course baseball - a sport we both love. Even in moments of silence, I realized I was happy to just be with him this way. It was one of the first times we were able to spend together since my return from India.

We arrived in the late afternoon to a little French-Canadian town surrounded by lakes and checked in to our Airbnb. It reminded me of a cottage in a fairy tale. Pine trees were lining the main street, there was a little spa down the road and three or four restaurants. Staying in the cottage of Snow White and the Seven Dwarfs, the comedy was not lost on us how romantic this place was and how out of place we were. The alarm clock went off the next morning and I swear I heard a rooster crow an hour earlier. I left Robert DeNiro to spend the day hiking in the provincial park down the street and I made my way to the training center.

The certification process is tough. When we went over the course breakdown, I felt like I was not prepared. Maybe it was self-sabotage, moments of *what had I done, and perhaps what I had not done*. Not only do you have to demonstrate your skills, but the most important part is how well you can teach your skills to others. You are marked based on your teaching ability and your knowledge of safety. For example, if a person fell off a board and had some sort of seizure or was unresponsive, how would we manage to get them safely back on? If a person is taken away by gale-force winds, how would we save them? Where was my Baywatch lifeguard now who saved me from that flying cockroach in India?

As we walked down to the water, I smiled, as it reminded me of the movie *Free Willy*. No whales of course but pretty close. Each person in the training had their strengths and weaknesses. There was a young buck in the course who was intimidating because of how talented he was. My advantage was that whatever I lacked in skill I could make up with my teaching ability. I was one of the better communicators, and I didn't shy away from doing skills demonstrations. But then it happened. It was time to Pivot.

Pivoting is primarily used in racing. YES, it's true. Paddleboarders race. This was not like Ross from *Friends* yelling pivot while trying to cram a sofa up a flight of stairs. It was worse. Pivoting is when you stand with one of your feet at the back end of the board and your other foot near the middle, putting all of your weight on your back foot, thus forcing the front end of the board high out of the water and spinning it very quickly, changing your direction in a few seconds. Pivoting in this course for me was what parallel parking is like for many when they first go for their driving test. It's a *must-do* and a make or break in passing the course.

I remember sitting there on the boards surrounded by trees with vibrant reds, oranges, and yellows, watching the others do their pivoting demos. This had been a hobby of mine for so long, but what if I wasn't good enough to pass? The fear was overwhelming. I put all of my eggs in this basket and it all came down to one moment. I felt like Kerri Strug at the '96 Olympics needing to land the vault. My turn came and I brought my board around, so I was in the center of the ring they all formed. I took one step, two steps back with my back foot on the board. The nose lifted and I placed my weight on my back leg and spun it 360 degrees in the air before setting it down smoothly. "Can they see how happy I am? Don't let on that you're so happy, because then they'll know," I thought to myself.

Around midday, the clouds rolled in covering the sun until it disappeared completely. The sky darkened and didn't seem so inviting anymore. As I leaned over my board, looking at the water, I could see droplets bouncing off the water. Then I saw the droplets on my board. I looked up at the sky and thought, "Crap, it's going to pour and I'm still going to be out here for another five hours." At one point the instructor said, "If you want dry suits or wet suits, we can go back, and you guys can suit up." I tried to hold off for a little bit, but the rain got so bad that we had no choice. We were falling into the water on purpose because the temperature was warmer than the sudden drop in air temperature. At that point, I knew I had to put on protective gear. The rain was coming down like pellets and it was freezing. The protective gear made us all look like astronauts going off on an expedition, but it kept us dry and warm. It brought me back to visiting relatives in England in winter. It's not at all like the dry cold we have in Canada or the U.S. It's a bone-chilling cold, the kind that stays with you until you can warm up in a hot shower. That evening I told my dad all about the pivot turn and how amazing it was, while we ate wings and drank beer at a tavern in the next town over, listening to musicians belting out the blues.

The second day wasn't much better weather-wise. The sun came out for a few minutes at a time in the morning, but for the most part, the sky was grey and rainy. We were better prepared for it this time knowing what the rest of the day would entail. So, we went out in wet suits at the very beginning. I just kept looking at the bright side - I would not ever be working in these conditions. Rainy days would be off-days and clients would be rescheduled. I knew what was coming and what I was working towards and that kept me going. Stormy weather and rough waters continued throughout the program but never broke us. It did make us question why we didn't do this in June rather than the last weekend of September - but it didn't stop us. If anything, it made me want it more.

Finally, the moment came. I was AQUAMAN! The feeling of completion was such a relief. The biggest hurdle I had to get past was now behind me. I was ready for take-off.

As we merged onto the highway heading home, I smiled at my dad and I looked out the car window covered in water droplets. I stared out at the tall cedars and pines lining the road and thought of how pretty they would look in a few months once they were covered in snow. It reminded me of my younger years when Dad would take me to early-morning hockey games.

When I was about six years old, my dad decided I was going to be the next Wayne Gretzky. So, he enrolled me in hockey as an extracurricular activity. To everyone's disappointment - even my own - I spent the whole season doing absolutely nothing! My dad spent his mornings getting me dressed in my hockey gear for forty-five minutes before, as well as forty-five minutes after every game and practice. It was more exhausting for him than it was for me out on the ice. At least he didn't have to worry about my hockey equipment being drenched in sweat or smelling bad. It was still bone dry by the time my skates were off the ice. Oddly enough, our team ended up making it to the championship that year. At the Championship game, I somehow found myself on a clear breakaway and scored my first and only goal! I was a defenseman who had never been past the red line. My dad was so proud that he still brings it up at Thanksgiving dinners. I guess it made all of those countless hours he spent getting me dressed worth it. I gave up hockey at the end of that season. It wasn't for us. Now we laugh about it as the time that I retired and went out on top.

My Dad turned to me and said, "Mike Shoreman, the Boardman." I replied, "Ha, Dad." "They're going to call you Mike Shoreman, the Boardman."

CHAPTER FOUR

Come hell or high water, this is happening. I set out to become: AQUAMAN.

For the next few months, I kept my head down and started planning. Winter was especially harsh that year, so I didn't leave home much. I just compiled data while drinking gallons of tea and being cautious of not starting my first season with a stomach full of baked goods. I spent hours and hours doing research, dissecting different business models, and taking bits and pieces of things I liked to incorporate into my own business. I became a student of how others operated. You might be surprised to know that there are over ten full-service paddleboard businesses in the Greater Toronto Area. It's crazy, competitive, and territorial. I did a full-on SWOT analysis (Strengths, Weaknesses, Opportunities, and Threats) of the entire paddleboard community. I stalked their social media and business reviews. I went through every single review that is out there and analyzed the shit out of it. I had charts and graphs; you name it. I knew exactly what I needed to do, what I wanted my social media to look like, where I was going to operate, and how I was going to position myself in the marketplace. I was going to differentiate myself as the one that put on a show.

Always factored in was a sunset lesson and tour on the waterfront in front of the skyline. Each student would get a dry bag to bring along a picnic dinner and after the lesson portion, we would all break for a picnic on land facing the city. This would be followed by a photo shoot of them lighting up the water like tea light candles in lotus flowers as planes descended into the local airport just above us.

Andrea and I met when I was in my mid-twenties. When she started cutting my hair, I got to know her and what I saw I liked. She was gentle, kind, and compassionate. She was also resourceful, intelligent, and savvy. When you meet people like Andrea you don't let them go. She never stood a chance with me and we became good friends. As our friendship developed, she decided it was time to open her own salon. A little before I went all *Eat, Pray, Love* on everyone, and shipped off to India to find myself, she said to me, "I think you need to do this, Mike." I think because she went through a business launch herself, she saw the potential. She knew that I would be good in this role of teaching others - having the power and responsibility that comes with working for yourself. We talked about what she went through when she opened her business. I was there, and I watched what she went through, but she guided me with her experience.

All of my equipment had been purchased before this. I also knew that I had to be certified by September to be up and running the following May. There were many boxes to check off before I could get started. And the frustrating part is the time it took to check off those boxes. But soon enough they would get marked off and all my days and evenings would be spent on the water.

The day the boards arrived was like Christmas. They were shiny and new, and I ripped through the packaging with sheer delight and growing wonderment. This was actually happening. It was beyond exciting.

The name came in the spring. I knew that I wanted to put 6 in the name, because of Drake and how he had coined Toronto as *The 6*. Also, I thought it would be catchy. I was aware that a lot of businesses had "SUP" (stand-up paddleboarding) in part of their names, and I knew I wanted to include it. Eventually, I came up with "**East of 6 SUP**". Easy. I threw it around to some friends and they liked it too. My family didn't. My dad was skeptical: "I don't know about this." But I liked it. I remember having the logo printed. It was the Toronto skyline with a paddleboarder paddling in front of it. The lettering was in a circle around that. It was all in neon, which I thought was important to reflect summer and fun. I was influenced by Venice Beach and Miami vibes, places to which I had previously travelled and felt reflected my spirit.

I also needed my driver's license. Yes, there was that. I knew I would need a license as well as a truck to transport my equipment. These boards weren't going to drive themselves. I'm going to be candid with you here. I was worried that I was not going to pass the driver's test because I am not a good driver. I never really was. One time while borrowing my dad's car as a teenager, I took off one of the side mirrors. For some reason, I thought he wouldn't notice. Or I hoped he wouldn't, and I could just blame it on someone else. But he must have known something was up or knew I was bound to do something because he checked the car over pretty quickly once I returned it.

"Where the fuck is my side mirror?" he demanded. I had been preparing my puzzled look for hours before I got home. So naturally, my acting skills came into play when I responded with, "Wait, what are you talking about?" It wasn't long before I folded and confessed everything. He definitely wasn't happy with me after that one. But hey, it could have happened to anyone, right? And it wasn't nearly as bad as the time my sister drove (with him in the car) straight into a field of bok choy. So, you tell me what's worse? He's probably scarred for life after that one. I doubt he's had any bok choy since that day.

I scheduled my test for the first day of May. I was worried the administrator would ask me to parallel park because it's like pivot turning - remember? I was also concerned I might take the side mirror off again in some weird twist of fate. But I passed. Barely. And all systems were GO! Two days later I bought my first truck, a previously used black Ford pick-up that drove fast and still has all the mirrors attached.

I did my first ever paddleboard lesson at Toronto's Cherry Beach in late May. At the time I remember thinking to myself that there wasn't any other board business operating there. I had my own first lesson almost a decade earlier down there, but that instructor was long gone. I knew there was room for something. There are two huge parking lots, mature shade trees, a dog park, a beautiful beach, a food truck, washroom facilities, and right around the corner is the entryway into the Toronto Harbour. You can paddleboard over to the Toronto Islands in about 10 minutes. This is prime real estate, yet nobody was there. *Why isn't anyone here in this location doing this?* Every other Sunday they had the Cherry Beach parties with DJs playing electronic house music - remixes of songs that we all knew. It would bring in hundreds and hundreds of people. I just remember thinking the summer before I got certified, "There is something special here." This perfectly conserved place was waiting for me to step up and take charge. In the spring of 2017, **East of Six SUP** was birthed right there.

CHAPTER FIVE

The dream is alive. I have built my own Atlantis.

Cherry Beach was almost too perfect, like a blank canvas waiting for me to create something truly spectacular. The fact that it hadn't been taken by another business was serendipitous. It was my personal tabula rasa, and I did it with every event I created. It was as if people came to dance on the water, lighting up the lake. I lit people up when they were going on first dates and falling in love.

On any given day you could find me wearing board shorts, flip flops, a fanny pack, hat (that I would wear backward), and my collapsible matte, black Ray-Ban sunglasses. I was in the best shape of my life, having lost about thirty pounds that summer because I was so physically active every day. I started my set up between eight and 8:30 am and would have pleasant, relaxing mornings with breakfast by the beach before unpacking all the gear. Some of the regulars came to know me. I would wave and greet them as they made their way past me with their dogs wanting to play with one another and sometimes wanting to play with me or sniff out the boards to make sure they weren't threatening.

It was June when I realized I had some competition at Cherry Beach. Another business had set up on the beach and was taking clients out. They had banners and signs and they were bigger than **East of Six SUP.** On a busy Saturday, the beach was taken over by both of us and we each had between six and ten boards spread out on the sand looking like planes lining up for take-off.

I watched people getting up on a board for the first time – growing anxious, nervous. Oh yeah, all those fears – those questions: is it going to be hard? Will I get hurt? And then the confidence once they are up. They are the candles. People light up once they master standing up and they develop a new skill, a new passion. My earliest lessons always began at 10 am. Then, the rush would start as clients raced in. Sometimes throughout the day, I would forget to eat as I was catering to calls: "Can we come today? Are there bathrooms? What should I wear today?" Days were long as I would wake up at seven am and not get home until after midnight. But it was worth it. I felt like I was giving people an experience that they would remember.

It wasn't always smooth sailing. There were the elements that had to be looked at every day. I always hoped for sun, heat, and low winds. I lived for that wind tracker. If the kite surfers were out, we were in. If we were out, they were in. But that also meant me getting on the phone and moving everyone to another day. All the other companies took it day-by-day and sometimes even one hour at a time, hoping for the best. I always stayed vigilant watching whoever I had out there with me. We weren't each other's enemy, strong winds were. That was something I initially failed to see when conducting my S.W.O.T. analysis.

For the first time in my life, I felt like I was in the right place, doing exactly what I was meant to be doing. I wasn't just teaching people; I was creating an experience for them; ones that were memorable and filled with excitement and fun. It was a powerful feeling knowing I had created that. I loved making people happy and hearing how much they enjoyed themselves.

With the sun beating down I would greet everyone with a handshake or a wave as they arrived. They were sometimes a bit apprehensive or unsure of what was going to happen, but by the end of the evening, I had people hugging me goodbye. It was a shift in our brief relationship which started just a few hours earlier. I would see people building relationships and new friendships on the water. These were people out on first or second dates that I still follow on social media and that are still together today. Sharing a sunset with someone is a very special thing. One of the greatest gifts of what I built is that it created space for these relationships to bloom. People would ask me, "Do you ever get sick of this?" My answer was and always would be, "Never."

I loved it. Why wouldn't everyone do this? Being on the water was where I felt most alive, and watching the sailboats go by or the swans ushering their babies away from us was like a parade at Christmas. This is life and it should be embraced and lived.

On the flip side, I found myself not relating as much to people close to me that were not business owners. Friends and family didn't seem to understand the hours that I was putting into this. I put a lot of pressure on myself because I was going at this on my own with very little guidance. I was trying to figure it out as I went. I lost so much weight that summer that I purposely gained twenty-five pounds through the winter going into the next season knowing that I was going to lose it fast. I felt like I was half actor gaining weight for a role and half fighter trying to get into the next weight category. But what I was doing was gratifying. Every minute I put in made a difference. Finally, I felt that I had something of my own. I was happy and fulfilled.

Eventually, as people started noticing more of what I was doing on the waterfront, I was asked to be the water safety expert for the Canadian Safe Boating Council. Delivering safe water tips and doing demos for the lines of media on the holiday May weekend was the perfect kick-off to the boating season.

I met Ben, who became my partner. He was a real guy's guy but super sweet at the same time. We grew close and he was like a brother to me. Tall, with blue eyes, he was the power boarder who did white water rafting and other adventures. Ben is the kind of guy that goes camping, portages with his paddleboard up over his head, sets up his campsite for the night, and continues on his journey throughout the day. He is very rugged, like a Bear Grylls type of man. When he saw what I had built (my business) he said, "Wow, it's like a whole show you put on. I want in." My business was like an Atlantis I had constructed. It was an experience for people, even more than dinner and a show.

Ben and I built a great relationship while he worked with me. I was not in any romantic relationship, so he stepped in as my work husband. He was a great companion. We bounced ideas off of each other and it worked well because he was very much the opposite of me in many ways. We were like Timon and Pumba (from *The Lion King*).

Very quickly I realized that I needed to do a lot of promotion for my dream to take off. This was not going to build momentum just through word of mouth, so I teamed up with several of the big blogs in Toronto such as *Toronto*

Date Ideas that had thousands and thousands of social media followers. We would launch contests throughout the summer to win a free date experience for one or two couples. Consisting of a three-hour lesson and a tour, part of the lesson was on land and the other part on the water. That allowed the student to feel completely comfortable on the board before we departed on tour. Halfway through the trip, we would sit down and have dinner on our boards in the open water. After that, I became the photographer, capturing their fun paddle boarding memories.

Sometimes I thought I was brilliant and other times not so much. One time a girl won the contest and showed up with her friend, who had sprained her ankle. And it wasn't just sprained, it was on the verge of being broken. She couldn't put any weight on it at all. She thought paddleboarding sounded like a great idea. So, she was just sitting on her bum for the majority of the trip. Looking at the wind tracker, I decided to take the group to a bird sanctuary - my back up plan for when it was still safe to go out, but the water was choppier than normal. As soon as we turned around to go back, the wind picked up out of nowhere coming straight at us. I didn't want to alarm anyone, but it was basically *Twister* out there, just without Helen Hunt and fewer cows and barns flying around. Canadians often complain during the winter, "Why do we live in a country where the air hurts our faces?" Well, it was July and this wind was hurting ours.

This would be the first and only time I felt lost out there. *Just how bad is this crossing that should take twenty minutes going to be? Is some passing boat going to call the Marine Police Unit on me?* I could imagine the conversation, "Oh Mike, so great to see you. We met at the Safe Boating Media Day…FML." I could see it on the front page of the newspaper. *This is going to be brutal.* Game face was on. All I had to do was paddle through *The Perfect Storm* on my 40-pound board and channel Mark Wahlberg. That's all I had to do. I attached the girl's leash to my board and pulled out a secondary leash and attached that to her board and my ankle. I got down on my knees. No, I wasn't praying. You have more power when you're on your knees and the wind is coming at you. The normal twenty-minute crossing took just over an hour with just me paddling. Yes, that's right. She forgot to paddle at some point!

From a very early age, I have been drawn to and also terrified of sharks. As a professional paddleboarding coach in Toronto, this wasn't going to be an issue for me. I have paddled and surfed in places where there were sharks, but I felt comforted knowing that whenever I went out, I wasn't going to be someone's dinner. When I was growing up, my family would drive down south for our vacations alternating between Florida and North Carolina. I was about ten when I watched *Jaws* for the first time. This was a traumatic experience that stayed with me throughout our entire trip and for several years after. I refused to go into the ocean for the next few weeks and I boycotted the pool at the hotel. You know those circular lights at the sides of the pool? I had it in my head that they could open, and sharks would come out and attack me. It's so crazy how imaginative kids are and what they can create in their minds. Things were different now. I had overcome that ridiculous fear of sharks. It was time to turn my fear into fun and market the shit out of it. Discovery Channel had been running *Shark Week* for years and it was time to bring some sharks to the Toronto waterfront. The world needed more sharks.

Shark Week SUP was born. I would wear a shark costume while teaching lessons and doing my tours, and people could get pictures with *The Shark* to post on their social media. There would be daily draws with prizes for all those who came out, a mix of swag donated by local Toronto businesses wanting promotion, and all the great Shark Prizes. I partnered with Toronto's *Ripley's Aquarium of Canada* which gave me tons of free passes to shell out to go see the sharks live and in person, and, wait for it…. *Warner Bros Canada*. It wasn't quite *Jaws* but in 2018 Jason Statham starred in the summer's shark blockbuster film, *The Meg*. Yup, everyone got bags and t-shirts and passes to see the movie. It was nuts and I loved every second of the craziness. It even caught the attention of Ian Ziering, best known for his role on *90210* and who also starred in the super cheesy *Sharknado* movies. Kids got certificates that said they survived *Shark Week SUP* and it became this happy thing that we all looked forward to. Everyone wanted crazy pictures with the shark on the paddleboard. It was truly "Jawsome."

Years earlier, I had a lot of fun during my first paddleboarding experience, but maybe not everyone else would. I spent forty of sixty minutes in the water partly because it was choppy but also because the instructor threw us right into the water with no real instruction. I knew that this was not the way to teach paddle boarding, so my approach was different. I gave a beach lesson first. People would be lined up taking instruction regarding the equipment, the boards' anatomy, and an outline of what was going to happen over the next two hours. Additionally, there was safety information to review before we got out on the water. It turned out well. People wanted to come back.

My evening lesson was billed as the *Sunset Lesson*, and it was always the most in-demand. Because of the sunset over the city skyline, all of the paddlers would leave with stunning pictures. By the time we got back to the beach, the sun would be down, and the temperature would have dropped. We always advised people that there was enough room in their dry bag for both their food and a sweatshirt.

I would have to bring all of the equipment up from the water to the parking lot. It wasn't that far, but I had to make multiple trips carrying heavy gear. That meant all the bags, all the paddles, and all the boards. Then I had to organize everything before putting it in the truck. I would often look up into the trees surrounding me in the parking lot and see little eyes glowing. They belonged to the raccoons living in the park. We started to become friends after a while. These raccoons were nothing like *Meeko* from *Pocahontas*. Some of them could be aggressive but mostly fine if just left alone. They would climb on top of my equipment, and I would have to chase them off. They climbed on everything and reminded me of doing the same thing as a little kid. They would get into the garbage bins near where I parked and get stuck in there. Then I would find something to lower into the bin so they could grab it and I would safely hoist them out.

Finally, the end of September rushed in, reminding me that not long ago I was in French-Canada eating pastries and becoming the captain of my own ship. The late September air was noticeably cooler, and the smell of pumpkin spice lattes now filled my truck. I finished with my last clients of the day and we said our goodbyes. The sunset paddles were now ending much earlier than six months ago. Hugs and thanks were exchanged. The last goodbyes echoed in the lonely night. After packing up the equipment I made my way back down to the beach.

How had the summer gone by so fast? I thought about what a perfect summer it had been and the magic of the water. How many times had we *lit up the water* over the last several months? I had turned nervous, awkward beginners into paddling warriors who were confident and sure of themselves and proudly raised their paddles high at the end of their lessons. *How did I get this lucky?* "Next year," I thought, "Next year will be even better."

My students felt the same:

- *Just went paddleboarding with three others and it was fantastic! We had very limited experience, but Mike made everyone feel comfortable and capable. We started at Cherry Beach and paddled over to the island. The view was incredible, and Mike took pictures, so we didn't have to. I highly recommend East of Six for anyone, whether you are experienced or novice.*

- *We did the daytime paddle, but I would love to do the sunset one - it sounds incredible! I planned this outing as a surprise for my boyfriend. Thanks, Mike, he loved it!*

- *Had a great time with Mike learning how to paddleboard. He does a great job of showing the tips and tricks and takes you out to fantastic locations. I took an afternoon lesson around*

Cherry Beach, the bird sanctuary for which Mike took great photos. Look no further than East of Six SUP!

- *Wanted to try paddle boarding for a while now and after yesterday's sunset SUP with Mike, I'm so happy I finally did it! From the booking, through information emails to the safety & training demos and the tour itself, the experience has been incredible! Mike is on top of everything; a true professional with a passion for delivering a great experience to all participants. Great location, stunning views, and an unforgettable experience! Can't wait to do it again!*

Throughout the summer, I began chatting with Erin. Erin is a paddle business owner based in Laguna Beach in Southern California. Her business, like mine, is built around the magic of sunsets and we formed a nice friendship of messaging back and forth. In October I traveled to L.A. to meet her in person and to figure out if we might work together going forward, offering paddle and yoga retreats in different locations. The trip was amazing. I felt like I needed more Erin in my life from the moment I met her. We spent time together on the Pacific. Our feet dangled off our boards into the ocean, as we watched dolphins and seals, and talked about what we did and who we were. I saw how she interacted with her clients and friends, and who she was as a mother and a boss. She left me feeling inspired and excited about working together the following April going down the Colorado River to the Grand Canyon.

When I landed in Los Angeles, I saw Guy Wilson, an actor, at the airport. He played Will Horton in the daytime television series, *Days of Our Lives*. We ended up having a great conversation. He had just come from India, so we swapped a few stories and experiences before departing. I felt like I had arrived in L.A. at that point. Besides getting into a fight with a famous adult film star named Wesley Woods, that was the scandal reel of my L.A. trip.

I planned to spend half of the year in California, the rest in Toronto. I thought, *this is just the beginning and things are only going to get better*. My dream was to be with people and share their experiences, and to hear their laughter lighting up the water, just as I had seen in India – lotus flowers and candles.

Soon after I got back from California after the second season of running my paddleboarding business, I hired a photographer and invited all the paddleboarders to come out and do a photoshoot of us paddleboarding inside the square fountain in front of the illuminated *Toronto* sign at Toronto City Hall.

CHAPTER SIX

The tsunamis in our lives that take us down all look very different.

It was November and I felt like I could finally breathe. Life slowed down for the first time since last April. My early morning starts were replaced quickly with leisurely lie-ins and my focus became the paddleboarding trip I booked that winter to Thailand.

I picked up a tea from Starbucks on a cool afternoon and drove down to the water as if knowing that this would be the end and that I was going to say my final goodbye. I pulled into the parking lot that used to be full and was now barren and empty. The washroom facilities were shut down and the dog park was quieter.

Making my way down to the water with my board next to me, I sat with my tea and took in the sounds and sights, listening to the gentle crash of the waves hitting the shore. I attached my leash and put on my lifejacket and rushed into the cold water that was up to my knees. Paddling out, I looked over to see the city skyline and watched the planes landing in the airport one right after the next. The clouds let up and the sun emerged, hitting the skyscrapers, and reminding me that the magic was still there even alone on a grey November day. I pulled my jacket in close to warm up and I said out loud to myself, "You have a lot of work to do in the next six months." I said goodbye and made my way slowly back to the shore smiling but saddened that this was goodbye for now.

Almost every Hollywood movie involves the main character first being placed in an unwanted situation, then resisting the call to action, and in the end, reluctantly assuming the warrior title. He goes into battle, loses the first round, often at the end of the first act, and ultimately survives but as a changed person. He shares that new knowledge with the world. This is called the *Mythological Journey* or *Hero's Adventure*. My own call to action was about to happen.

The writing on the sign at the desk was black. *Please present your health card and one other piece of government-issued identification.* The walk-in clinic was unusually busy for an afternoon and I worried that I was in for a long wait.

The pain began the day before, but I had managed until now to combat the assault with extra strength pain relievers. "This is different," I thought to myself. I sat waiting and waiting, searching my mind for a possible cause or link to what I was feeling. I stepped outside notifying the girl at the counter I'd be right back and called my mom to tell her where I was and that the pain I told her about last night had turned into something now unbearable. Ushered into the doctor's office, I was led to the examining table and told that a doctor would see me shortly. I sat in silence thinking; *I wonder if this is going to go the same way as when I broke my arm? I hope I get something to alleviate this feeling and get back to normal.* The door opened and the doctor entered the room. I felt disappointed that this wasn't a McDreamy from *Greys Anatomy* kind of appointment. We went over the basics, and I said it began as a headache that got worse and worse and this pain in my ear was now intolerable.

"Were you travelling recently?" I was asked. "Yes, I was just in California." I went over the details of my trip saying I was surfing and paddleboarding on the Pacific just a few weeks ago. He proceeded to look into my ear for some seconds. Once finished, he spoke, "Likely, this is a really bad swimmer's ear or dirty water infection." *Makes sense. Although I've never had swimmer's ear before.*

That night my mother asked me if I wanted something to eat and offered to go get dinner or to make me something. Standing in the kitchen, the only thing I wanted for dinner was a bottle of extra-strength pain relievers. I bent down to the floor and placed my hand on my ear to protect it, wincing in more pain than I had ever known. I said goodnight to her and thanked her for accommodating me and, fighting back the tears, went to her spare room at the top of the stairs. I hardly slept that night. It was like the most painful abscess in my mouth had made its way to my ear and I was ready to Van Gogh it right off. I woke up exhausted and doubled up on two pain relievers, taking four pills every two and a half hours to combat the pain, thinking, "This isn't right, something isn't right here." I had no working nerves on one side of my face.

Two days after the trip to the walk-in clinic, I broke down and thought, "I cannot do this anymore." I got in the truck and drove myself to the emergency room and noticed that I was having bouts of dizziness while driving. The streetlights seemed off and the lanes on the roads narrower than usual. The same questions were asked of me as before about my travel and what I was experiencing. A light was flashed into my ear and just like that, we were done. I was given a prescription for an antibiotic and I was out the door, on a mission to get to the pharmacy as quickly as possible and save my ear.

Cut it off. I don't care anymore, just take it right off.

I spent the next few days on the couch drifting in and out of sleep with the TV playing in the background. The pain of a now red and swollen ear too tender to touch woke me up. I tried repositioning cushions to get as comfortable as possible but nothing worked.

By the end of the week, I had cancelled plans with Andrea to go away for her birthday to a ski lodge. I was in tears while on the phone with her. Not because I was desperate to go skiing or because I was letting her down but because I knew this wasn't ending and I felt like no one understood the pain. Nausea swept in and I spent nights racing to the bathroom huddled around the toilet, praying for this to stop. I was trying to negotiate deals out of desperation with whoever is upstairs to just stop all of this.

It was Armistice Day, November 11th, 2018. My foot hit the floor and I knew it wasn't right. I had to lean on the wall beside the bed to push myself up. I staggered across the room and fumbled with the doorknob. It seemed as though the door would never open. I felt like I was still in a dream state, a nightmare as I made my way down the stairs in my pajamas. Clasping the banister with my hands, I felt drunk and my vision was off. The fifteen familiar stairs in front of me seemed like a maze I had to navigate ever so carefully. My mom heard me and came out of the kitchen with her coffee and said, "We need to go to the hospital right now."

She gently guided me over to the wall mirror showing me that my face had collapsed on one side. I didn't recognize myself. I looked like I had a stroke overnight, but I was too exhausted to break down. The pain was out of control. I realized I couldn't blink my eye on that side, and I didn't know what was worse - not being able to walk properly, or the constant throwing up. The excruciating pain was beyond anything I had ever experienced. We got dressed and she guided me out the door, letting me hold her arm as I made my way down the driveway to the car. I turned off the radio as the sounds were amplified and I couldn't stand the music coming from the speakers. I leaned my head against the side window and looked out, not caring if anyone saw me or how I looked.

We arrived and I projectile vomited all over the manicured hospital lawn before being led into the building. I was triaged at a level two. (That's a big deal. You should take note of that.) When a patient goes into the hospital, they triage and rate them somewhere between a one and a five based on the symptoms. You have to get shot or stabbed to go in as a one but being a level two, the doors opened quickly for me.

I was dehydrated, so was I put on an IV drip. They decided to give me valacyclovir in the drip and sent me home to continue treatment and receive home care. A nurse would come to my house and teach me how to use and change the IV. Eventually, I was wheeled out of the hospital in a wheelchair, feeling exhausted and relieved that this was now coming to an end.

Spoiler Alert: this was not the end.

The nausea got worse as if I was having some sort of allergic reaction to the very thing that was supposed to be making me better. I was stumbling like an alcoholic in the depths of despair, trying to make my way back to the couch from being sick. A puke bucket was finally placed beside me, so I did not have to make trips to the bathroom.

Two days following this ordeal I found myself entering a new hospital, the final hospital. My ear was now swollen, bloody, and black from pustules that had formed and ruptured. Within minutes, I was ordered a CT Scan and blood work to determine what was breaking me down. This was the first time anyone mentioned anything about testing. Following the scan and bloodwork, we were sitting in a waiting room, my home IV still attached to me. A woman sat across from us. She was the kind of person who needs to talk all the time. She told us we were in a good hospital and that they once saved her from flesh-eating disease. My mother tried to make light of my situation and whispered to me while quietly laughing, "See, at least you don't have flesh-eating disease." I just looked at my mom like, *What the fuck?* As if this wasn't bad enough, now we had this woman to deal with.

We were called upon like students waiting to see the principal. The doctor led us down a hallway that never seemed to end, where I sat down in an examination chair, exhausted, out of it, but ready to take whatever was coming. "The tests have come back and show that you have a reactivation of the chickenpox virus from when you were a kid. It has attacked your ear. When shingles attack your eye or your ear in this way, it is called *Ramsay Hunt Syndrome.*

My mother was shocked and so was I. I was also extremely jealous that she could show emotion on her face and that I couldn't express my shock.

He then asked how it all began. I told him about the walk-in clinic, then the first hospital, and then the second hospital, and about all of my symptoms. His mouth opened wide in disbelief. "You see, with Ramsay Hunt Syndrome, there is a 72-hour treatment window. You're the third case of this I have seen in here in the last month or so. I'm going to put you on an intensive steroid treatment, and we will see what that will do but there are no promises." I suddenly turned into Sherlock Holmes and put two and two together. "Does that mean we can take this IV out of my arm? Because it's just making me sick." He smiled and said, "Yes of course. Someone will come and remove it in a few minutes." He was very gentle, probably the gentlest doctor I have ever met. Kind, compassionate, and empathetic towards what I was going through, he was the way all doctors should be. He just could not make sense of how this could have happened and why tests weren't run until after the seventy-two-hour mark.

Before I knew it the toxic IV was removed and we were on our way out, on our way home to navigate whatever this new normal was going to become.

Robert De Niro took me to the next appointment as I was unable to walk properly and needed someone to support me. I was put on medication to fight the vertigo. The spins in my head made me feel like I was on a rollercoaster. The medication sometimes worked and other times not at all. When vertigo hits, it is scary. It's like someone has pushed you too quickly and you're lost in it, trying to come back to where you were. Then, you are so relieved when it stops but also you are anticipating it coming back and taking you again.

In early December I was scheduled for an MRI. This outing did me in for days, exhausting me of any energy I had. As my dad guided me down the hallway of the hospital to the lab, he asked me if we were walking too fast and it saddened me to realize that my life was going to look very different. I couldn't even bring myself to look him in the face. He led me into the dressing room where I slowly removed my clothing and put on a hospital gown, worried about the fact that I couldn't blink my eye. "What if there are lights in there that zap me and then I lose my vision - it's already obstructed in this one eye. Will I be able to hold my eyelid closed or will that not be allowed?" I lay down on the machine that reminded me of a rocket. As I was being told how the MRI worked, I got that pull feeling from vertigo. It was like someone pulling my head back and then spinning it like a basketball. I asked them to stop. We waited until I was settled, and the noises of the MRI started.

In general, Ramsay Hunt Syndrome is exhausting especially in the first months, even years. It's a neurological condition, a chronic condition. When the doctor asked me in those initial appointments what I did for work, I told him that I was a professional paddleboarder with my own business. His response hit me like a freight train. "Oh boy." That was all he could muster up to say. I had never heard of this syndrome and everything I was hearing about it was breaking news to me and to the people in my life, the ones I was letting in. Also, my late diagnosis held no promises of a future recovery. This disease affects people in very different ways. Some people have mild cases while others have very severe cases.

Leaving the MRI appointment that cold rainy December night, it hit me. *The magnitude of all of this and what it meant for me.* While driving home, my dad asked if I wanted something to eat. I said, "I think I'd like a sandwich from Subway," looking out the window avoiding his eyes. *It's done. Everything I have worked for is done. My business is done. It's all gone.* I felt like sobbing with despair as I brought my fingers to my face to cover it. He left me to cry, touching my shoulder, and returned a few minutes later with my dinner and a pile of napkins for my tears. "You don't know that it's done," he said.

Getting through December was rough for everyone in my family. There was sadness, anger, and rage. I went through my days exhausted from this new beast I was living with. When I was awake and alone, I was not who I was before. There was no magic, no spark. As the weeks led up to Christmas, the trip to Thailand was cancelled and my life turned into one defeating appointment after the next, trying to find something that would make any of this better. I broke down at the slightest thing. I was a shell of who I used to be. Looking in the mirror became a painful reminder of what was. Washing my hands, I avoided looking at the monster staring back at me. I took my time moving slowly from room to room feeling like a prisoner in my mom's home with no escape and no hope as reality crept in. Sobbing into the sleeve of my robe alone in the bathroom, hiding what I was going through, and hoping no one would hear my pain. *Who is ever going to want to be with this?* My verdict was to semi-live a life sentence of sadness.

Cats by nature do not look happy. However, Max, aka, "Pants" has been my biggest buddy from the darkest days. He's a fluffy, long-haired, black cat without much of a personality. He cries when you walk in the door. It's all verbal. But if you're lying down on the couch, he climbs up on the wall behind you and lays himself around your head or your heart. And he's usually asleep. It looks like he's got a little lion's silky mane. When he comes home from the groomer, he's very self-aware of how exposed and naked he is. And as his fur starts to fill in, it looks like he's wearing little furry pants. So, I just started calling him "Pants" instead of his name, Max. Even in that time of being home, he was in the room with me, and I think that animals - even cats who are aloof - can sense when something's wrong. Just having him there meant that I wasn't alone.

It was usually my mom or dad who called to check in, or my friends would call. I would never go out of my way to call anyone. Sometimes I would talk to Pants. I believe that animals like to be talked to. Pants would start crying for me to give him wet food in the evening. He gets dry food all day and then he gets wet food in the evening. He starts crying for it or he'll go and stand by the doorway into the kitchen and start crying. And the crying turns into a mournful cry. It's oh, so dramatic. He sounds like he's dying from starvation, yet his bowl is always full of dry food. After he does eat, he passes out in a food coma – sprawled out on his back. He's a trusting cat, and sleeps with arms over his head, legs up straight north. Then he wakes from his slumber and marches back to the kitchen and starts crying again because it seems he's forgotten he already had his dinner. I think he's trying to manipulate me into giving him more food. It's just a game with him.

Those were my days. Pants and me. Sometimes I believed he genuinely cared about me and my condition. "The cat has empathy," I thought. But then I would hear his cries and think, "No, he doesn't. He only cares about the condition of his stomach."

CHAPTER SEVEN

This didn't just affect me. It took a heavy toll on the people all around me. They did their best not to show it because they knew I was the one suffering, but when something catastrophic happens to someone, it affects everyone.

By Christmas, it had been decided that I would spend ten or so days in the middle of the month at Robert DeNiro's house to give my mom a break. She needed to see her friends, have a life of her own, and work overtime which she needed because of all the time she had taken off. I was asked by everyone if there was something I would particularly like to receive from "Santa" this year. *A new face*, I would think to myself. I had decided to enjoy this Christmas as best as I could and to try to be as happy as possible knowing that this might be the last holiday I would spend with my family.

I am usually a festive person. I look forward to seeing people and the food, the laughs, and the opening of the brown paper packages tied up with string. But this was different, and we all knew it. When I arrived at my dad's, he brought me and my bags in and sat me in the living room by the tree. The fireplace was on and I heard laughter in the other room as my family wandered in one by one greeting everyone. "I should be in that other room," I thought to myself. But I was not myself. I was embarrassed and shy and the confidence I had to look people in the face was gone. I was relieved and anxious, scared even when my sisters came to join me by the fire and saw me for the first time. Everybody knew about what was going on with me, but I don't think they expected it to be as bad. Seeing my face and the way that I walked was a big shock to everyone. There were tons of hugs and people asking me how I was and if I needed anything. I asked them how they were and what's new like nothing had happened. They told stories that kept me entertained and I tried to look at them, seeing the sadness in their eyes. I snuck off to the bathroom, locking the door behind me, and sat down on the floor with my knees up and my hands and head resting on them, processing all of this.

We opened presents and I received a little more than the rest, something that hasn't happened since I was in my early years. But the thought of it was nice. "Maybe I should have my face collapse every year if this is how it's going to be,"

I briefly thought. I was excited to see their faces when they saw my gifts to them. Thank god for online shopping. When it was all said and done, the living room was covered in wrapping paper and the dogs were hunting for the cats hiding underneath. Beside me were seven pairs of new track pants and sweatshirts. Everyone was determined to keep me comfortable through my crisis.

We moved into the dining room and the feast began. We all wore crowns pulled from Christmas crackers and everyone was into the wine except me. I kept my head down for most of the meal. I was happy to be there but did not want to be seen. The evening continued as I was opened up to the world of board games that had never interested me before that day. The game was about building your town and getting resources and I was hoping my sisters would let me win because I needed that, but I was unapologetically swept by every single person in my family. Dicks!

I have never really felt sadness around Christmas before - only once was the magic stripped away. When I was seven or so there was a big storm in Toronto. The snow was coming down so heavily that the school called all the parents to pick up their children. We didn't even make it to lunchtime. I had no idea that there was a big panic as to who was going to pick me up from school. So, either my mom, my dad, or my stepmom was to show up. I guess my dad got the short end of the stick because he picked me up and brought me to work with him. Everything was going well. I was enjoying my time at work with him that day. I was working hard on my Christmas list for Santa and at making Christmas drawings on the cards I was to give to each of my family members. My dad's boss came by and asked what I was doing. I told him, beaming with excitement. "Christmas list?" He responded with, "Santa's not coming this year. Your dad's not getting a Christmas bonus." I was traumatized, to say the least. My dad walked in and I told him what happened, and he was so pissed off. His boss was just joking, and at my age now I would definitely find that funny. But at the age of seven, I questioned Christmas unnecessarily.

Christmas for the Shoremans wrapped up and appeared to be a success. I even managed to laugh a few times and was grateful that everyone came together. I stayed on this little high through New Year's surrounded by my parents, distracting myself with movies and way too much candy. Just after Christmas, I tried to go out of the house a little more. I saw how people reacted to me and it made me uncomfortable. The looks I received in grocery stores reminded me of the freezer aisle where everything was like my heart and soul, blocks of ice.

The way my family talked to me was another concern. It was like I'd retreated into a younger version of myself and people spoke to me in a gentler way. After all, when something like this happens, people who love you want to be compassionate and caring. I picked up on the way people looked at me and the way they flocked to me and I remember thinking that that's how they see me. I know it was all in my head, but you think the world sees you this way. When I looked in the mirror, I wondered how I would ever be able to go online to find somebody to connect with. Every box is filled with a sea of lonely torsos and they're all just gorgeous. And then I have this face. How would I find somebody who would love that? Do I try to go online at some point and post my real picture, saying, "Oh, I fell down the stairs," and hope that they understand, or do I just post a *before* picture? There was no point. And I wasn't ready for sex or being intimate with somebody and was not in a place to go on a date or to be in a relationship. My thoughts were running into "Who's ever going to love all this?" So, I put my time into personal development and there wasn't much left for relationship building.

On Boxing Day, Robert took me downtown to a store in the Beaches to exchange some of the wrong sized sweatpants I had received as gifts. As we were walking into the store, Gudrun came in. When she realized it was me, she was shocked and said, "Wow. Mike!" I had met Gudrun just after I got back from California after my second season of running my business. She had contacted me online last fall saying she wanted to be a part of the photoshoot at Toronto City Hall. Now, I was wearing a patch to protect my eye, holding on to

Robert DeNiro with my left arm, using a cane, and trying not to fall because the sidewalk was crazy. It was one of the first times I had bumped into somebody that I knew. It threw me off. I was going through extreme dizziness and vertigo, and I was very conscious of how my feet hurt. Gudrun had heard about what happened to me and asked me how I was doing and if I needed anything. The conversation went on longer than I had hoped. It felt like a million years at that moment because I was so uncomfortable. I didn't want to be around people, and I didn't want her to see me that way. We were business competitors and had only met one time. But she was kind. I could feel that. She has continued to support me throughout my RISE.

Then January continued and so did the eating of bad food and watching crap on TV. My life became watching *Days of Our Lives* and trying to figure out how John and Marlena were still together after all this time. Everything felt like a battle. Moving from the bathroom to the living room was exhausting and I felt like my relationships were dwindling because I had lost my independence. My untouched truck was parked in my mom's driveway buried under a foot of snow and I couldn't bear to go to the window and look out at it. I retreated and avoided going out, not wanting to be seen by anyone, even strangers.

I had an appointment to take place in March with an ear, nose, and throat specialist. He was going to give me recommendations for vestibular rehabilitation therapy which helps retrain the brain to walk normally. But following a trip for more testing at a balance center (yes, that's a real thing) my dad and I felt that the wait was too long, and we had to get started on this therapy right away. During one test, they brought me into a room where there was a machine with a red laser that moves from side to side. My job was to follow the red line with my eyes. I would spin out in the attempt. Another test had me laying down on my back on a bed and they would pour what seemed like a gallon of water into my ear and tell me to count backward from a certain number.

"I can't even count forwards right now, what are you doing to me?" I remember counting down from 20 to one, and by the time I got to number 13, I just spun out, feeling like I was holding someone's hand while wearing hockey skates and them whipping me around. The guy that ran the clinic came out and said, "So what are they going to do with you?" He sounded like I was fucked. I just looked over at my dad, defeated.

When I first went into physiotherapy, I had lost all my confidence and self-esteem. I didn't want to be in a room where anyone would be looking at me. I was wearing sweatpants and walking with a cane. It's not a great look for most. Shane did some testing and was gentle with me. He said that he had never worked with someone with Ramsay Hunt Syndrome, but he is a specialist in vestibular rehab therapy and that is a requirement for treatment. He instructed me to do walking exercises. I would walk two steps and put my head up, and then walk two more steps and move my head down, each time feeling like the ground was moving underneath me. Then, walk three steps and turn my head to the side, and walk another three steps and turn my head to the other side. I loved seeing Shane but every time I'd leave feeling deep shame. It felt like I was doing all of this work yet was not seeing any improvement.

This is a great time to tell you all that I am a big believer in rewards. It started in my childhood. I remember as a kid having to go to the dentist to get my retainer put in. I was actually so excited. Not to get my retainer in, but because my mom made a deal with me that I could go see the new *Jurassic Park* movie afterward. My excitement was through the roof. I had even bragged to everyone at school about it. Unfortunately, my mom was not able to take me after my dentist appointment, so I went back to school with my tail between my legs. All the kids swarmed me with anticipation of my movie review. I was like "Oh yes, it was really great with tons of dinosaurs," and immediately went to my seat. So awkward.

But I was getting rewards for going to physiotherapy. It quickly became a tradition that following my sessions, Robert DeNiro and I would head off to see a movie. It would be my one big outing for the week. My dad would lead me into the theater and sit me down in a place where I felt hidden and protected, usually off to the side, and then he would disappear only to reappear with popcorn and candy and all the bad stuff. A little "You crushed it at physio- here's your reward." We saw good movies and a lot of bad movies. I didn't even care what we saw, it was just nice to be out of the house and have a change of scenery in the middle of the day when no one was around.

By February I started doing short trips to the grocery store with my mom. I would be holding onto the shopping cart for support and moving slowly, but I was determined to get my own food. If I wanted a certain type of fruit or ice cream, I wanted to be able to get it myself. But seeing people's reactions to my face and how I was moving was crushing. I could see them questioning what was wrong with me. The stares and the looks of pity I got made it worse.

CHAPTER EIGHT

It was like the waves wouldn't stop crashing and I just kept being knocked down. Anytime I tried to get back up, a bigger wave would come. The pain. The humiliation. The self-hatred. The loneliness. It had been days, weeks, and months. My world had become tiny.

Blades of brown grass stuck out from the snow as I looked out of the window. The foot of snow on my truck was gone and I should have felt happy that spring was coming but I knew what was ahead of me. I had to announce that I was closing my business. I wouldn't be paddleboarding anymore. Grabbing my cane, I walked slowly back to the living room and sat in silence for ages, thinking about how I was going to explain this to others. I wanted a glass of juice but the trip that normally took me seconds now took a lifetime. I got up slowly and pulled out the juice jug and a glass and began pouring only to fumble the handle and drop the jug onto the tile floor. The sticky sweet juice surrounded me and my now soaked socks. Alone, I raged as I slipped on the juice and crashed down on the floor. This was not my first fall and it would not be my last. I swore out of anger and frustration as I mopped up the contents in that jug intended for me. I thought, "Everything is going to be harder from now on, but it doesn't need to. It could just end."

That was not the first time I had thought of taking my life. It had been going on for three months now. Daily thoughts ran through my mind, usually when I was left to my own devices. If only they knew what I was thinking. I would probably be locked up in a padded room so as not to harm myself. The 2018 sequel to *Girl, Interrupted*: "Boy, Interrupted." I thought of the different ways to do this, the ones with the least pain and those that would be easiest for my family left behind.

It was April and I was looking out of a huge window in the doctor's office when he told me my life was over. He began with, "What I'm about to say is going to be devastating considering what you do." He went on to explain that my life of paddleboarding was no longer a reality. People who have my condition have a really hard time looking at water or being around water as it makes them feel dizzy and nauseous. If I were to go on the boards, I would probably be sick afterward. Flying was also going to be challenging with the air pressure changes. Plane rides were out. Road trips were out. It was all going to look different from now on. Tears streamed down my face as I tried to hide my misery from my dad who sat beside me. I left that appointment a complete mess.

"That dickhead doesn't know what he's talking about," Robert DeNiro said. But inside I knew the doctor was right. I began to emotionally shut down and didn't say another word the whole way home. My dad knew I was devastated, and he didn't have much to say. In January, he had tried to encourage me by suggesting, "You can rebuild this, and I will help you." He offered to help me set the business up for other people to operate under my supervision. But that wasn't what I wanted, nor was it something that seemed very realistic given the state I was in.

Left with the devastation of the news, I awoke the next day only to find it was sunny outside - yet all I saw was darkness. It was as though the world had a light shone upon it, but I couldn't seem to escape this cave of shadows. I felt like I was walking alone in an endless dark field of thick stalky grass. Every time I took a step, my footing was unstable, and I struggled to see more than an arm's length in front of me. There was no way out. The world was happening outside my window, and people were going about their normal lives, but I just could not get into the stream of life that seemed so effortless for everyone else. I used to strive to be the best at what I did in my business. Now I would do anything even for mediocrity. Just to get off the couch, get properly dressed, walk out the door, and have somewhere to be. I was exhausted from doing this day after day and felt like I was completely unrecognizable to everyone in my life, and most terrifying of all, to myself. Sitting alone each day, I was fading away from the world. I know what I was supposed to do. I was supposed to lean on the people around me, but they seemed so far away. At this point reaching out for help was a task far too exhausting. Even if I could, I did not want to be a burden any longer.

I made my way downstairs to the empty living room. My mom had gone to work for the day, and I was relieved that I was alone. This meant I did not have to pretend that I was okay. I turned on the television and spent the next hours lying on the couch, drifting in and out of sleep while taking in all the sadness that is daytime programming. I looked forward to naps because they helped pass the time. Exhaustion was part of my condition. I thought, "What has my life become?" I received a few calls throughout the day. The names and numbers popped up on the caller ID, but I sent them to voicemail. Many of those calls were from my mom. She would call me every day from work, often twice a day. She asked me questions like, "How is your day? How are you feeling? Do you want me to bring you anything? Is there anything that you need?" Then, she would tell me about her day and ask me what I was up to. I would always reply, "Napping and watching TV." My condition was physically exhausting. My appetite had decreased to zilch. I did not feel the need to feed myself. What fuel does a person who doesn't do anything, actually need? I didn't feel that I deserved to eat. I was withering away. I felt powerless over time, and the days slipped away from me slowly. I realized that I had manifested the lyrics of the song *Cosmic Love* by Florence and the Machine which have replayed many times in the past months: "But then it stopped, and I was in the darkness, so darkness I became." I felt the utter emptiness of being entirely unloved and unworthy. I was dying of loneliness and despair.

I decided this would be my last day. I had toyed with the idea since before Christmas. During the holidays I thought this would be my last. I called my mom at work and told her that I planned to stay at Andrea's place for the night. Otherwise, she would worry. I told her Andrea offered to pick me up and bring me over for a visit. I needed a break. It sounded like a reasonable enough plan and so she took me at my word. She was frankly relieved and happy to hear that I had made plans to get out of the house and see a good friend. I could tell by the sound of her voice that she was grateful to Andrea. I knew that would be her reaction. We said, "Goodbye, see you tomorrow, or maybe the next day." and ended the call.

I slowly made my way upstairs to my room to change and get ready and started my shower process. This meant sitting in the bathtub with a stream of water coming down on me like a waterfall as I held my eyelid down since it would not blink on its own. Otherwise, the water would hit my eyeball. I washed with my other hand as best I could, fumbling with the shampoo bottle and then the slippery soap bar. I got dressed for the first time in months, trying to make myself appear presentable. I had been going to appointments, the grocery store, and generally out and about (very rarely), in the track pants I received for Christmas. For this mission, I knew I needed to make myself look like I was somewhat okay. But I was not at all okay. I thought that if I could dress up somewhat, I could pull it off. So, I put on jeans for the first time in the longest time. I struggled to get them on. It was like putting on skinny jeans for the first time in five years after you have gained weight. I was dizzy as I shimmied back and forth to try and get them on. My head felt like Jell-O in a bowl being shaken around. Finally, I was ready. I grabbed my cane and my coat and said, "Goodbye." to my home.

Now I was on a mission to get the stuff that I needed. I was aware enough to realize that I needed to present myself as normal, although my state at that point was anything but. I was using a cane and others could tell there was significant nerve damage in my face. I started downtown, making my way to the train station and catching the next available train to Union Station. It was already dark outside, which gave me comfort. Finally, my surroundings had begun to mirror my feelings. That feeling expanded as I approached the person who had the stuff. Finally, it was time.

When I had it in my hands, I knew that I dared to go through with my plan. I would just numb myself until the gaping emptiness that continued to grow inside of me would be no more. I would *be* no longer. I would be too fucked up to think about anyone else, not about my mom or Robert DeNiro. This was the only way out. I was frozen before the stuff even had a chance to enter my bloodstream. It was somehow already controlling me. My movements were almost robotic as I proceeded to step deeper into the darkest night. This stuff is supposed to be the quick elevator up and out of the darkness. It promises to provide you with wings and is the solution when you cannot see any other way. I felt I could only go one way - up. I planned to go higher and higher until I just slipped bravely away into the darkness.

I found some company. They had a balcony. It looked like the perfect place. They did not know my plan or else I am sure they would not have agreed to have me over as a visitor. We carried on into the night. I slipped away into a daze and for the first time thought to myself, "Life is better blurry." How odd, considering it had plagued me for so many months but in my current state, it was oddly comforting. It was not the elevator up that I had hoped for but I continued to dive deeper into oblivion. I came to in the hallway. My back was against the wall. I was told to put my hands behind me. I tried to find words to speak but I was so out of it. One of the officers said, "Your face..." I struggled to respond, "Ye-e-e-ssss.

Some-th-th-ing h-a-a-a-pened." He asked, "Now?" I replied, "No. A few months ago. I have a-a-a neurological condition. A-a-a-nd m-m-m-y face collapsed. It wasn't from th-th-th-is." And he said, "Okay." with compassion. I asked if I could sit down and pull out my hands. He said that would be okay. There were five of them around me. Eventually, we walked downstairs. They asked me what I wanted to do next. At that moment, with my feet planted firmly on the ground, I realized I was still here. The thought of the last day was gone. All I needed was to deal with the circumstances that I was facing at this very moment. For the first time in a very long time, I needed to do the next right thing.

They called an ambulance to take me to the hospital. There were a lot of questions. They checked my blood pressure and breathing, made sure I was hydrated, and checked on me several times. I was very out of it the whole time. When my vitals were okay, they released me. It was now early in the morning and the sun had just begun to rise.

I decided that I needed to go to Robert DeNiro's. I had to take another step forward. I got in a cab, gave the address, and proceeded to head northeast to his home. The scenery became greener and lusher as we exited the city. Even the air was different. It was cold, as winter had not yet decided if it was fully ready to make an exit. We stopped at a red light on a city street about five minutes away from his home and I spotted a family of geese ahead at the opposite side of the road, beginning to make their way to cross in front of us. Momma goose stepped out first, babies in line behind her, and Papa Goose was in back keeping watch over them all. They moved quite slowly since the babies were tiny. They were not running. Neither was I. Even if it was tiny baby steps, I was starting to make them in the right direction. I thought of Robert DeNiro and how he saved me from the geese when I was young. I ran and flew up into his safe and loving arms. It felt like I was doing the same, only now as a thirty-something-year-old. Although somehow, I was more in touch with little Michael now, more than ever.

I knocked on the front door and Robert DeNiro answered in his robe. He knew instantly. He could see it in my eyes and in my face. He was broken-hearted, and this made him furious. We went inside, sat down, and proceeded to have the most significant talk of my life. I told him everything. He asked me, "Michael, what do you want your life to look like? Who do you want to be? Do you want to be this person? Or someone that people love? Because whatever this is, it is going to lead you down a path where you will lose everything. Your family. Your friends. You will live on the street. Everything that you hold dear will slip away. So, who do you want to be?" I took it all in. It felt just like those safe hands that saved me from the angry geese so long ago, but this time I was being rescued from something inside of me. Something that was desperate to take me down. We hugged.

Then, I spent the next hours sleeping and sweating out the last of the stuff.

When I woke up, I felt mostly back to normal. Robert DeNiro drove me home to my mom's and said that we had to tell her. I watched her heart shatter. She said, in tears, "I didn't realize that this is where we were." She didn't understand. "I don't want to be here anymore," I said, "I just don't want to do this anymore. Everything I built is over. The car trips with friends and Dad are not possible for me because I will be throwing up the whole time. Going on a plane will affect me for days." Robert DeNiro grasped his hands together, his head down toward the floor as tears streamed down my mom's face. I continued, "This is not the life that I was supposed to have. I have been thinking about ways to end it since before Christmas." They needed to know this was not a new feeling. This was the catalyst. "You need help processing this." Mom told me. "You need some help with the sadness, grief, and loss." "Sure." I sniffled. "We are going to find somewhere for you to go," Robert DeNiro stated. "But you have to go," Mom cut in. "That is a condition that we are making for you to stay here at home." My eyes welled up with tears. "Okay," I agreed. Mom hugged me, Robert DeNiro hugged me, and then I slowly began to make my way upstairs to bed. "I am so sorry," I said, halfway up the stairs. "We know," they both replied at the same time. It took me one and a half minutes to get up the final half of the stairs. I could hear them talking softly in the living room. I knew that in the morning he would be back to take me to the next appointment, which was probably going to be even worse than the last.

Robert DeNiro was there on time to take me to my appointment downtown. That was the day they tested the nerve damage in my face. In January and February, I did a lot of research on my condition so I would be familiar with all the terminology that the doctors would use when discussing nerve damage. During the appointment, I had plugs on my face zapping currents into it to see if the nerves were responding. The doctor stopped and said to the assistant, "Okay, see here, there is definite evidence of synkinesis." And I knew that this meant the nerves weren't responding or repairing themselves. That appointment was my last shred of hope. Although I sensed what the outcome would be, until I heard it for certain, there was still a chance that things could turn around for me. Now I knew they wouldn't.

When we left that appointment and got into the car in the parking lot, I broke down, exhausted. "I can't go on like this anymore," I cried. Robert DeNiro looked at me and said, "We are going to get you some help." That evening Robert DeNiro drove me to a crisis centre. We went home for me to pack a bag - but I didn't even know what to take. When we got to the crisis centre, I said goodbye to him and as the car door shut, it echoed for what seemed like forever. I watched as he drove off before making my way slowly to the front door.

I was greeted with smiles and kindness from the staff as I checked in. I felt dizzy for the first time this week, probably brought on by exhaustion. I was told to change and given temporary clothes while they washed all of my belongings - a standard procedure to avoid bed bugs. I was thinking they probably wanted to make sure I wasn't bringing in anything to harm myself or anyone else. Once changed, I passed my clothes over to be washed and was given a tour of the home. I thought I would sleep downstairs with the guys but I lucked out. I was given my own very small room. There was a dresser, a side table, and a bed with one pillow. I was led back upstairs to be shown the backyard, the kitchen, and the living room space. We walked into the office to talk about why I was there, and I was surprised that I was not pushed to give more information than I was willing to share at this moment. We went over the rules of the house – curfew, lights out time, and expectations of me. Leaving the office, I poked my head into the living room, and I saw a hockey game on the TV and thought of Mom and Dad who were probably both watching at home. I sat alone, conscious of what I was wearing, as a support worker joined me. I was not very talkative, and she sat in silence with me as I watched the puck being rushed down the ice back and forth by the teams. As I headed to bed for my first night, I was told that I would have my clothes tomorrow so I would feel more like me again. "Whatever that means," I thought to myself.

I woke up and remembered where I was. I stayed in bed until there was a knock on the door. "It's time for your room check," said the nurse. And at that moment, I knew this was me hitting a low. I moved slowly to let her in as I stepped out, not wanting to watch her go through my things. Upstairs there were people watching TV and some were eating. I grabbed some bread to make toast. Then I headed outside to the backyard where there was a gazebo and I sat with my thoughts. I was interrupted by others who came out to smoke and get fresh air. Then I went back inside, pressing the intercom and looking up into the video camera, showing them, I was waiting. My clothes smelled clean and were folded for me, and I was grateful to have my stuff back. I took a shower and sat down in the tub with the water shooting over me like a waterfall. When I finished, I slowly stood up and made my way back to my room avoiding anyone, shutting the door behind me, wondering when I would get my next room check.

The following day I woke up on my own and felt more rested. I interacted with others in the house a little more. By the third day, I felt comfortable talking to the staff about what had happened to me and why I was there. The conversation wasn't forced and as far as I could tell it seemed to be on my terms which made me feel like I had some control. I also ventured out that night for a short walk down the street to a Burger King, which was disgusting, by the way. It has to be my least favorite of any fast-food restaurant. I ate my food slowly knowing that when I headed back, I would probably be staying in for the rest of the night.

On the fourth day of my crisis stay, I opened up to one of the women working there. I told her how I felt alone and like my life had been taken away. There were tears as I left to sit outside in the cold under the gazebo. I noticed the birds chirping for the first time that year and decided it was time to call Andrea and Ben and tell them where I was. Ben had checked in on me during the cold, long, harsh winter when I was struggling, and I actually answered his calls.

As my stay at the crisis centre wound down, I was set up with a mental health counsellor once a week in addition to my sessions with the psychologist who would help me process my experiences. As I said my thanks, I was grateful to have a place to go, even though I was anxiously thinking about what being home again was going to be like. I was looking forward to having the comforts of home but super stressed about the reactions of my family and what I had put them through. Before going to the crisis centre, home was dark and depressing and I did not have a routine or any structure in my life. At one point I wasn't even getting up and showering. I needed a new routine and I needed help.

The purpose of the crisis centre was to help put some structure back into my life and break down what I was feeling. When it came time for me to leave, I felt stronger in the sense that I didn't feel hopeless anymore. I had a path now and that included talking with counsellors and therapists. I knew I could not do this on my own and that I needed support. That support was the foundation that would lead me out of the darkest headspace I have ever known. Therapy helped and provided me with the tools, but it was my job to do the heavy lifting. There was still sadness, yes. I was a realist and knew that life was not going to be rainbows and unicorns once I left. It was my job, my responsibility, to come to terms with my situation and process it in a healthy way. I needed to start letting go of the rage and grief that consumed me. So much resentment and anger toward the medical system, the doctors, the hospitals, and friends and family. Everyone. Eventually, the rage and the anger subsided into sadness, and that sadness is what I needed help escaping. I had a big realization in that period with the councilors when I learned; *I'm the one that has to do this work.* It was a lightbulb-going-off moment. I knew I had the help of those people and I was grateful that they were there. Truly, I just had to buckle down, get serious about my life, and turn this around.

I had faith that the line from *The Dark Knight* was true, "The night is darkest just before the dawn." And there was nothing left for me to do, but RISE.

CHAPTER NINE

When facing rough waters, we have two options: SINK or SWIM.

When I returned home from the crisis centre I felt a deep shame. I was sorry for what I put my parents through. My guilt was heavy as I thought of how I had let them both see me in that state and how our relationships would never be the same. I had shown them everything. Would they always see me in this shameful way?

I started writing a list of fun things that I could do during the summer. This exercise was to help me balance out the lows that were bound to hit me when the paddleboarding season began and all the businesses would be out doing their thing and that just wasn't my reality anymore. The list would be of things I could look forward to. Lana Del Ray's *Summertime Sadness* was my theme song at the time, but it didn't need to be. "Kiss me hard before you go, summertime sadness." So sad. So, my list included things like BBQs, moving my vestibular exercises into pools, going to the theatre, and watching the sunset. I would go to the local pools to do my exercises in the slow lane with the grandmas. I started going outside again for really short walks in my neighbourhood to watch the sunsets. Sunsets were a huge part of my life. I finally felt like I had some hope again.

In April I started to take things seriously with my physiotherapy, finally seeing a big improvement. I would go home more committed than ever to do my homework. It consisted of studying all the therapy images and how to do the exercises properly. And I started seeing results. I would go into my physiotherapy sessions and try the exercises without using the cane. My physiotherapist, Shane, really started pushing me in a way that I felt comfortable and safe. He would always be there to catch me or to take breaks when I felt that I needed to. He would say things like, "Wow look at you today! You are so much better than you were last week. See, must be those exercises!" I had a lot of shame initially after leaving the crisis centre. I didn't want to talk about it much, but Shane knew about my mental health struggle and always made sure to let me know he was a safe place to go if I ever needed to chat.

I started doing my research to help normalize what I was going through. I picked up my iPad while visiting my dad and typed in "famous people with Ramsay Hunt Syndrome." I thought, if I can put a face I recognize to this, then maybe it will help me process it. Up popped two politicians. One I recognized and one I didn't, and Tony Horton from P90X. Tony is an author, personal trainer, globally recognized fitness guru, and creator of the commercial home exercise regimen P90X. That Tony Horton. I found a few links and they led me to an interview he did on TV's *Extra* about his journey with Ramsay Hunt Syndrome. I decided to contact him. I don't know why, but I knew I needed to. I wanted answers. What did I have to lose?

Tony responded to me in days. I was shocked. We became Facebook friends and we talked. I learned that our common condition had put him in a wheelchair, and he still found himself struggling, years later. We did check-ins and we continue to have great life chats. He normalizes the pain and the grief I'm going through. We became friends. He wrote to me, "Mike Shoreman - Hey my friend, we fight on! Exercise was impossible for me for many months, but now it's how I improve. It's a real struggle some days, but I try not to judge it. Before, you were a great Paddleboard Instructor. Now you're an inspiration to others and catalyst for change in their lives." I felt like I wasn't the only one anymore. I joined a Facebook support group where I found over two thousand other people just like me going through all the things I was.

Days after notifying my social media audience that I wouldn't be operating my business, I was sitting at home when an email popped up asking me to be the water safety expert again for The Canadian Safe Boating Council's Water safety week's media day. I closed my laptop and called my mom to tell her about this. I thought about it a lot. For days. *How can I still do this? How can I make this work?* Later that afternoon I sent messages out, feelers to my friends in the paddling community. I told them that I'd been asked to be a part of this again and what's happened. I wanted them to be a part of this day with me, and to hold me up if it should come to that. I got "yesses" from Ali and Sarah within minutes saying they were both in and so excited. It was time to say *yes* to myself again, to stop putting these limiting beliefs on myself, and to say yes to life whatever that might look like. I think we all have a moment when we must make a decision in our lives. Do we stay where we are, or do we choose to step bravely into something new?

I worked hard on the relationships that I had cultivated while operating my business. I loved collaborating with people and learning from them and being a part of something exciting. This was what I was determined to do. There were so many amazing things about Media Day. The weather cooperated, we were all excited to see each other, there was press coverage for all of us, but the greatest gift came as the media was leaving and cars were exiting out of the parking lot.

Sarah looked at me and said, "Are you ready, buddy?" while grabbing my hand and leading me toward the water where Ali sat on a board waiting for me. Exhausted, I said, "No. I'm not going out there." "But you'll be with me and I'll stay here right beside you. You got this." And then it happened, I said *yes* for the third time. I let Sarah help me on the board. I was sitting on my knees as it was gently pushed out - Ali right beside me. Even though it was just for a few minutes and sitting down (vertigo hit me forcing me off the water), I felt like me again as the sun reflected off the water hitting my face. Something I had loved and lost had been returned and I was home after travelling for years. I was exactly where I was meant to be.

A few months earlier I had been out running an errand with my mom when we passed my friend Patrice's office. I remember that day vividly because of what she said to me. Dressed in sweatpants, using a cane to support myself, I made my way into her office. It was the first time she had seen me since my new life took over. I felt embarrassed whenever I saw Patrice, still uncomfortable with people seeing my face. I removed the eye patch that protected me from the wind, and this fireball of energy embraced me gently and asked me how I was coping, and how was I feeling. "What's up next?" She asked. "You're my friend, but are you okay, have you been on the wine?" *It's 11 am,* I thought to myself. She caught my attention with this brief statement, and I will never forget what she said next. "I know you, Mike Shoreman, you are not done and whatever this is, you will overcome it. I know you. There is a thing called *Speaker Slam* I want you to take a look at." "Hm," I said. "Tell me about it."

"It is Canada's largest Inspirational Speaking Competition and I'm going to send you the info. You have a story the world needs to hear. This is not the end for you, my friend."

CHAPTER TEN

I found out sitting at my dad's kitchen table in early June that I had been selected to stand on stage and deliver a powerful six-minute talk to three hundred people at Canada's largest Inspirational Speaking Competition. I was shocked. I had applied thinking, "Sure, why not?" when Patrice sent me the info a month or so ago. I'm not even joking when I tell you that I screamed, and I lost my shit when the email came up. Robert DeNiro was in the kitchen pouring a coffee and had absolutely no idea what was going on, but he was excited that I could get so enthused about something.

Suddenly I had a sense of purpose. It would be something to keep me busy aside from daily physiotherapy exercises and making my way to my appointments, now mostly on my own. "I wonder who I will be up against?" and I looked through the speaker's catalog and realized that I was not qualified. These were professional speakers with experience. Those who have gone viral with millions of views, some who have stood on stages with much bigger audiences than three hundred people. Some had delivered Ted Talks and had speaking businesses and I have given a couple of uncomfortable/awkward TV interviews about paddle boarding and water safety. I was in way over my head and I felt my lunch coming up. I was totally not prepared for this.

Three hundred and fifty – 350. That is the number of times I had rehearsed the speech out loud. For the five weeks leading up to the event, I spent three hours every night going over my script. I kept reading it out loud until I memorized it. I would use a high-low-high speech writing technique to bring the audience on a journey with me, painting a picture of what life was like before, and then the crash, and then lift them up. Surely a few people out of three hundred would like it. This audience wanted to be uplifted and inspired. "They aren't going to boo me, throw rotten fruit at me, are they?" I was full of fear that I was going to be filmed and that someone might see this. My heart sank when I found out that we would be filming at night when my face is the most distorted from the exhaustion of the day.

When I arrived at the event space, it was buzzing with people whizzing past me. I greeted Rina, who was the event organizer and co-founder. I don't think I had ever met someone so happy just to see me arrive. Composed but stressed, she told me where the washrooms were in case I needed to get changed, and pointed me towards Dan her business partner to help me out with questions. I had questions. I needed to ask Dan if there would be a chair on stage for me to hold on to, so I didn't lose my balance and trip in front of three hundred people.

Four tables of guests had come out to support me. Friends, family, and people from the paddling community showed up. My mom, her best friend, Robert DeNiro, my sister Hilary, her husband Peter, Gudrun, Ben, Andrea, Sarah, and Patrice. They all showed up for me. I think they were more anxious than I was. The lineup was announced, and I was the sixth speaker of the evening. During the intermission, I went outside into the alleyway beside the building and paced back and forth, repeating the first three sentences of my speech over and over. I felt like a figure skater who's at the Olympics about to wipe out on my third jump. Why did this have to be inspirational? Why couldn't I be some kind of Tonya Harding and go take them all out and then just jump on the podium?

As I opened the doors to the venue, I walked into the speaker's prep room and they put the headset on me, and I was given instructions on what to do next. I stood there until I was given the cue to move to the side of the stage where I met Rina who offered me a lemon wedge to bite on. She told me that it would help avoid the dreaded dry mouth and articulate my words on stage more clearly. But also, I thought they liked to see the faces we all made. My name was announced, and I climbed the stairs slowly onto the stage and took my place. Blinded by the lights, I couldn't see past the first few rows of people, which was a huge relief. The only things I could make out were flickering candles atop the tables, reminding me of the lotus flowers in India. I was pretty sure I could make it through this without peeing my pants. Except I wasn't wearing pants. I was wearing a suit blazer and board shorts so if I did pee myself, I was screwed. I began.

They called me Shoreman, the Boardman. I am a paddle coach with Paddle Canada. I teach stand up paddleboarding in front of the Toronto skyline. I teach beginners on the water, often nervous at first.

A lot of – "I don't-think-I-cans."

A lot of – "I'm not sures."

But eventually, those "nos" turned into "yeses".

At the end of my lessons, I would line my students up on their boards with their backs to the city.

I was ready to capture their moment.

With the sun setting and the planes landing just behind them I'd say, "PADDLES UP!"

This moment celebrated their power, their confidence, and was THEIRS.

But it was also mine.

You see, I built my own Atlantis on our waterfront.

I became, AQUAMAN!!!

(laughter)

I take great pride in building others up...

(I felt myself losing balance, so I grabbed hold of the chair set for me onstage and sat down)

...and sharing my passion in keeping others safe out there.

Being on the water is where I feel most confident – most alive.

And then it hit.

The biggest wave.

I didn't see it coming.

Eight months ago, today, as a thirty-five-year-old, my chickenpox virus from when I was a kid reactivated in my ear.

When shingles attacks your eyes, your ears, it's called – Ramsay Hunt Syndrome.

It's rare.

In a very short period of time – five days – my life altered.

A medical misdiagnosis.

A missed seventy-two-hour window for treatment.

Caused damage to my fifth, seventh, and eighth cranial nerve.

Facial paralysis.

Vertigo.

Dizziness.

Speech and vision problems.

Permanent hearing damage.

Pain said to be worse than the shattering of kneecaps.

But the scariest of all, I lost my sense of balance.

I have been in vestibular rehab therapy retraining my brain to walk normally, ever since.

On April the second of this year, I sat in a specialist's office with tears streaming down my face.

I was told, "this is going to be devastating considering what you do."

Your paddle boarding, no longer a reality.

The tsunami that hit me from behind five months earlier, now taking me down.

As this was being said I could feel the oxygen leaving my lungs.

The water now filling them.

The pressure of this crushing me.

I couldn't breathe.

I was drowning.

I closed my business. The lights faded.

The colour of my eyes went from blue to grey.

It is now the reality.

I am the Unbalanced Paddleboarder.

My mental health deteriorated very quickly.

In the mirror for months, I saw a monster.

I did not want to be seen in public.

I did not want to run into people at the supermarket.

And just two months after that I would find myself entering a mental health treatment facility.

I need help processing everything.

Sitting at home a short time later an email came through from the Canadian Safe Boating Council asking me to be their Water Safety Expert for their Media Day.

A year earlier I had done water safety for a line of press as long as this stage.

The lights came on.

The colour of my eyes, grey to blue.

I had to reach for this lifeline and say yes.

I called my friends in the paddling community and I said, please come help me.

And they said, yes. Of course.

A day of exhaustion. It was awesome.

And then my friends asked me to test the waters.

Get on a board for the first time.

Only months earlier I had been forced to switch from showering to sitting in a bathtub with the door open.

Bathing in a swimsuit in case someone needs to rescue you is scary.

To spin out as if on a carousel of terror while simply leaning back to rinse your hair only to come up and vomit all over yourself is TRAUMATIC.

To know that you now have to have another bath and do that all over again is HORRIFIC.

That day I said YES for the third time.

I lasted three nervous minutes sitting down on the board that day.

And let me tell you as a thirty-five-year-old guy who has needs, it was the most satisfying three minutes I've had in the last year!

(laughing and cheering)

I have been paddleboarding several times since that day.

I have even stood up for short periods.

The tsunamis in our lives that take us down all look very different.

When facing rough waters, we have two options – SINK or SWIM.

Saying yes again brought me back up to the surface.

When we say yes to ourselves just one time – yeah, just once – it makes it easier for us to say yes to ourselves the next time.

Two yeses became THREE, and three became FIVE,

And before I knew it, I had stopped saying no to myself.

Things may look different when we get back up to the surface.

But as you gradually start saying yes to yourselves more and more you will feel that crushing pressure go away.

The water now rushing out.

The oxygen filling your lungs again and YOU WILL BREATHE.

YOU'RE STILL YOU.

PADDLES UP!!!

(cheering, and more cheering)

As the speech ended, I stumbled backward from the Paddles Up motion I made with my arms towards the audience. When I stepped back into position, I felt like I was being pulled by a hand behind me and thrown like a curveball. As I stepped off the stage, I saw that Rina was crying and I hugged her before walking to the back of the room to have the microphone taken off. It was at this moment I realized the audience was all standing - something I couldn't do not so long ago. As I walked through the crowd, hands reached out to congratulate me and faces came towards me to say, "You did it, you blew the roof off." I knew at that moment I had done something special that would change things and inspire people to be the best versions of themselves.

I had never seen my parents look at me the way they did when I got off the stage. Robert DeNiro was ready to cry. My mom was grinning ear-to-ear. I was supposed to walk through the balcony to the back and get my mic off and then go out and hug everybody. My mom could not wait for me to do that. She grabbed hold of me tight and squeezed me harder than I think she ever has before. While the judges were deliberating in the back, I grabbed Andrea and stepped outside to get some fresh air. "You did it! You brought the house down," She exclaimed. As the third-place and then second-place winners were announced, it sunk in. I had just won Speaker Slam - Canada's largest Inspirational Speaking

Competition - with my story, using my words on courage. As my name was announced, the crowd stood up again and I was overcome with emotion and gratitude for the people who had stood by me and been a part of my journey.

The next day I awoke to find that my social media had exploded with messages of congratulations from family, friends, the Ramsay Hunt, and the Paddleboarding communities from around the world. We released the speech on Facebook late that afternoon and watched it gain over 35,000 views. People thought that this was important and that this message mattered. Friends, family, people who I had never met, were sharing this speech to the world. Sharing it, wanting their people to see it as if it was their own. An amazing thing happened. When I started going viral on the platforms and getting millions of views, the paddleboarders started raising their paddles in support. Hundreds of them from 48 countries and 36 American States posted photos, raised their paddles to the sky to show power and confidence, saluted the message as a gesture of support to people struggling with physical conditions and mental health challenges - whatever that looked like.

I remember waking up one morning, checking my phone, and seeing a notification on my Facebook page that an amazing woman, Nicki Day from Australia had tagged a post to my wall. She had asked her local paddleboarding club to take a picture of them at an event with everyone raising their paddles in the air. I couldn't believe it! There were so many of them. People I had never met on the other side of the world in a completely different season, on a different continent, were saluting this message. She tagged that to my

wall and signed off with the hashtag *paddlesup*. The crazy
thing about tagging on social media is that when someone
tags you, it runs through your feed and anyone can see it.
Other paddleboarders who saw my social media blow up and
saw that post wanted to be part of it. A paddleboarder in
Maine U.S.A. saw what Nicki had posted and created
a *paddlesup* picture and tagged it on my wall and
hashtagged *paddlesup*. And then Dani Burgess from the U.K.
saw what was happening on my Facebook page and got her
club to do it, and then John Knippers in Tennessee took one
and tagged my wall. Giufo in Italy and Sarah Thornely in the
U.K. did the same. Paddles Up posts flooded in from New
York to California, Massachusetts to Texas, Colorado to New
Hampshire, inspiring people in the paddling community and
around the world. People in Norway would see what
someone in Texas was posting on my wall and they wanted to
be a part of it.

Every time that happened it fueled the fire and
motivated other people to join in. Hundreds, maybe
thousands of paddleboarders from all around the world were
raising their paddles - watching and wanting to be a part of
this crazy thing. Sometimes the pictures would be in rivers or
creeks and sometimes they'd be in the ocean or in front of the
Eiffel Tower or the Hoover Dam. It triggered a tsunami, a
wave of community support from around the world that was
a thousand times more powerful than the tsunami that took
me down. It was a reminder to those who saw them what the
paddling community was all about: love, support, and
solidarity. Every day I continued to wake up to messages or
new tags on my social media pages, "We, stand up paddle

boarders, are standing up with you in this." Within days, my speech was picked up by Ashton Kutcher's platform *A Plus* and went viral for the first time. And then it debuted on the *Power of Positivity* to its 33 million subscribers triggering a tsunami effect through the paddling community. It brought people together that might not have otherwise met.

I had no idea when I gave my talk that I would win that night but the greatest gift to come was the millions of people who watched it and loved it - the comments, the hashtag paddles up posts, and emailed private messages. There were posts every day from people all over the globe celebrating their power and their confidence for people who couldn't yet do it themselves. Then the speech was turned into a mini-movie with Innerlight Media with images and music and was released on social media. It was reposted by motivational speaker Jay Shetty, gaining 650,000 views in a few days. The paddling community lit up social media like fiery lotus flowers and I felt like I was coming full circle and had hope again.

I sat down with my mom at the kitchen table and she asked, "How is everything going?" "It's going amazing, Mom. Everything is great." "You know," she said, "Your dad and I had conversations before you made your speech. We were worried about you and what would happen if things didn't go well. We were not sure if you were going to be able to handle it if it didn't turn out well." "Really?" I said, baffled. I had not thought about this, but it got me thinking, *it had only been a few months since my stay in the crisis centre.* I could see why they may have been slightly (hmm) concerned. Although, for me, it seemed completely normal. I felt totally in my right flow.

This was just like little Michael having pointed at something, got it, and then running up to the refrigerator to find a free magnet to display yet another proud achievement.

As an aside, I am reminded of the work done by Mihaly Csikszentmihalyi, considered one of the co-founders of *Positive Psychology*. He was the first to identify and research flow.

"The best moments in our lives are not the passive, receptive, relaxing times ... The best moments usually occur if a person's body or mind is stretched to its limits in a voluntary effort to accomplish something difficult and worthwhile." (Csikszentmihalyi, 1990).

One day I walked downstairs wearing a pair of grey shorts. I was moving slowly enough that my mom noticed me going and what I was wearing. "What are those?" I told her that they're just shorts. "Well, where did you get them?" "I got them last summer." "What store?" I said, "I'm not telling you because I know you and I love them." She smiled, and I said, "You are not getting these shorts." Yeah, I'm not doing "US Weekly's Who Wore It Best?" with my mother, and she started to laugh. As I say, I think it's bad enough that Dad and I showed up that one time wearing the same shirt. I'm not wearing the same shorts as my mom. She burst out laughing.

A great mom is a solid mix of the two best kinds of love, soft and tough. On the outside, we share the same blue eyes, blonde hair, and a pale complexion that seems fragile but hides a depth of character that still awes me. As I see my mom now, I am surprised at just how close we have grown over the past while. In my mind, she has become a very real

3-D version of the woman I once thought I knew. She hadn't changed – I was now understanding her better, and seeing her for who she really was, a caring woman who had sacrificed so much to help take me to this point in time. We had gone through the storm together and were now coming out the other end, hand in hand. We were in this together. Love is a word I do not use lightly and much of that was, and is, from son to mom.

In October 2019, I attended a speaking summit called *Archangel for Dreamers and Visionaries*. One of the speakers I met was Elizabeth Gilbert, the author of *Eat, Pray, Love*. I stood nervously to the side for an introduction. As we were having our photo taken, I told her how much her memoir *Eat, Pray, Love* had changed my life. It was one of the initial reasons I wanted to visit India. And the whole time I was there I couldn't help but feel that I was having my own *Eat, Pray, Love* experience. I was running away, but also towards something at the same time in order to bring something home to give to the world.

This is the part of the book where I am supposed to leave you with some wisdom and lift you up, motivate you and inspire you. I hope that by now, I have lit a fire inside of you. We have all felt at one time or another like we got hit by a bus. Something that took us down unexpectedly. We have all been through life experiences that have changed us, but it's how we respond and act that determines what comes next. When I talk to people about my journey, my lived experience, I say what happened *with* me. Not what happened *to* me. My mindset changed as my recovery progressed, and I navigate that. Do I still have bad days? Yes, of course. I also have good days when my symptoms flare up, and I crash, but I know I will get through because I have gotten this far. I have built myself to where I am now.

My Mom says, "Life is a series of peaks and valleys at different points." Highs and lows that we all go through. The highs are incredible, and the lows make us appreciate the highs even more. I hope this book inspires you to keep fighting- not give up on yourself, take chances, and rely on the people around you.

The global movement that was birthed in the experience of winning Speaker Slam was transformative for me. Not everyone reading this book will have that same exact experience. What I want you to know is whatever you are going through when reading this, fight, fight to get on your stage. Maybe for you, that means getting back to work or getting a new job or trusting yourself and someone else and falling in love again. Your stage is where you are going to shine, and you deserve to shine bright.

My relationship with Tony Horton from P90X has taught me a few things. When I initially messaged Tony, although I hoped, I never thought I would actually hear from him. He has hundreds of thousands of followers, a business with millions of people who follow him. Why would he respond to me? But he did. We never know who is going to react or how or when, but it does happen. We are all connected. We are all human, and nobody is untouchable. Nobody out of reach. Nobody. Not Tony, not me, not you, not Elizabeth Gilbert. We are all people.

Lastly, we have gone long enough without bringing STAR WARS into this. I'm surprised there hasn't been a revolt by you, the reader, because of that. I think it's incredibly valuable when looking for support in whatever you are going through, whether it's personal or business, to seek guidance from someone who has walked the road before you. In my story, I am Luke Skywalker. In your journey, you are too. Tony is my Yoda in many ways. He gave me answers and imparted wisdom on me. Go out and find your Yoda. Get the answers, guidance and support you need to make the best decisions you can with what you are up against. You are your own biggest advocate. No one is going to fight harder for you than you. Finally, remember when you get knocked off your board and have run out of steam but can see the shoreline off in the distance, get back on your board and finish the race. Finish *your* race.

ACKNOWLEDGEMENTS

This writing process has been similar to that of the original speech I delivered in 2019. Writing this book for you has been an emotional journey. A cathartic and healing experience that has reinforced my belief that we all have messages that can make people think, make people question, make people act to better their lives and the lives of others. Every one of us has a purpose whether that's lighting up the water or lighting up the world in other ways. I need to thank some people because I did not get to where I am today on my own.

To my parents, who I love. I feel like I won the lottery by getting both of you. I didn't just get one, but I got two superheroes. My Superman and my Wonder Woman. You have always been loving and supportive of my endeavors and have championed me in whatever I do. If I didn't have you both as parents, who knows what would have happened to me? You taught me the lessons and you were patient with me while I failed and learned them. You never gave up on me and you were there for me in my darkest hours. You fought for me when I didn't have much fight left. You are the real "SUP"er heroes in all of this.

To my family who never let me win at board games and who showed up for me when I needed you, I will forever be grateful that you were there for me.

Without the guidance of my mentors, this never would have unfolded the way that it did. You believed in me when I wasn't quite there yet.

Patrice Esper, you're the greatest mentor I've ever had. You forced me to dream big again. You pushed me into something so unfamiliar knowing I would land on my feet. Rina Rovinelli, you took a chance on an unknown, believing in my story with Speaker Slam. You and Dan Shaikh opened doors for me to a new world and helped me create a new life. The friendship with both of you and your encouragement has meant the world to me. Gina Hatzis, the *too much* woman. Who knew we would be here today? You probably did because you are wise, and you push the boundaries of what is possible every day. You are one of the most talented and gifted coaches and speakers I have ever worked with and I am in awe of you.

To my editors Richard Campbell and Brenda Rogers who took my manuscript and brought it to places I could not have on my own. Your mastery of the English language and your knowledge and skill have transformed my book to unimaginable heights.

To my publisher Tabitha Rose at *Life to Paper Publishing* and your team, I knew you were special the moment I met you. You believed in this project and the messages of my story when we had that first meeting. You made this dream a reality for me and I will forever be grateful for your work and your friendship. You crushed it!

To my team, you were the wind pushing me toward the finish line while this book came to life. Lisa Kirbie, Nesh Pillay, and Leona Burton you motivated me and inspired me. Thanks for all your efforts.

Figuring all of this out would have been impossible without great friends, Andrea Thompson, Ben McEwen Katie Bushie, Adam Bistrovich, Kathleen Izzard, Ashley Lynn, Gudrun Hardes, Emily Russo, Max Russo, Julian Ganton Tanja Semenuk, Adrienne Rommel, Sarah Powell, Ali Stevens, Blake Fleischaker, Dave Anderson, Alexis Dean, Diana Lee, Matthew Arbeid and Jovana Borojevic. I couldn't be luckier to be surrounded by such amazing supportive people. You all rallied for me. I'm a pretty lucky dude.

And lastly, thank you to the communities I am a part of. These include the amazing warriors who inspire me every day from the Ramsay Hunt Community, the mental health communities, and the international paddleboarding community who showed me love, support, and kindness.

And finally, thank **you,** dear reader.

ABOUT THE AUTHOR

MIKE SHOREMAN is a former professional Stand Up Paddle Boarding Coach, until in 2018 a neurological condition forced him to retire from the sport. Mike made the transition to consulting and speaking where he shares his remarkable story and the life lessons learned along the way. Mike is an ambassador for several non-profit organizations and a mental health advocate who fights to break stigmas. He is the winner of the 2020 SUP MAN of the Year Award and the International People's Choice Paddleboarder of the Year Award.

To contact the author, visit www.mikeshoreman.com

Mike Shoreman waving to children along the banks of the Ganges River, Varanasi, India.

Paddlers raise their paddles up in the air at the end of Mike's lessons in front of Toronto's stunning skyline.

Mike paddling through Toronto City Hall, October 2018.

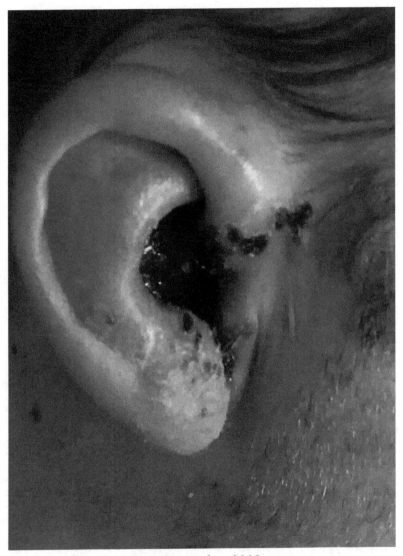

Ramsay Hunt Syndrome, November 2018.

Ramsay Hunt Syndrome, November 2018.

Ramsay Hunt Syndrome, 5th, 7th and 8th Cranial nerve damage.

Protecting eye from wind and dust particles avoiding further damage.

Mike's first time back on a paddleboard. Sitting down May 2019.

Mike standing up for a few minutes at a time with Ben, July 2019.

Mike delivers his 6-minute speech called "Paddles Up" / "I said Yes" at Speaker Slam, Canadas's largest inspirational speaking competition on August 6, 2019.

Mike thanks the audience of 300 and his supporters in the crowd after winning Canada's largest inspirational speaking competition.

Lake Mac SUP Club added 14 new photos.

12 mins · 🌐

What a perfect morning for our first Point score race for the 2019/2020 season, well done all, here's a few pics, more to follow **#paddlesupmike**

👍❤️ You and 4 others

❤️ Love   💬 Comment   ↗ Share

Paddles up from Australia.

Dani Burgess ▶ **Stand Up Paddle Board Newbies Group**   •••

9 minutes ago · 🖼

Paddles up **Mike Shoreman** ✌️ this ones for you 🙃 all the way from Alderford Lake in Whitchurch, UK 🇬🇧

❤️ Love   💬 Comment

Paddles Up from The U.K.

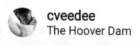

cveedee
The Hoover Dam

⋮

♥ ◯ ◁   ▢

 Liked by **quaylt** and **others**

cveedee 🔥 HOT DAM! Checked off another bucket
list paddle that i've been planning to do for a w... more

Paddles Up from The Hoover Dam.

courtoutdoors
Gudvangen

 Liked by **ben.a.mcewen** and **others**

courtoutdoors PADDLES UP from @supnorway in support of Mike Shoreman @eastofsixsup ... more

21 minutes ago

Paddles up from Norway.

Paddles up from Tennessee, USA.

Paddles Up from the U.K.

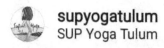

supyogatulum
SUP Yoga Tulum

❤ ○ ▽   ◻

 Liked by **tanjasana** and **others**

supyogatulum Today's post is dedicated to our
amigo @theunbalancedpaddleboarder querid... more

Paddles Up from Mexico.

Ozark River Walkers is in **Ozark, Missouri.**

25 mins • Ozark, Missouri • 🌐

#PADDLESUP for our Canadian Brother **Mike Shoreman - The Unbalanced Paddleboarder.** You are a huge inspiration, Sir!

 You and 5 others

💗 Love   💬 Comment

Paddles up from Missouri.

Paddles up from Italy.

Paddles up art from Scotland.

Mike Shoreman, "The Unbalanced Paddleboarder".

Coming full circle with Elizabeth Gilbert author of Eat, Pray, Love at Archangel Summit, November 2019.

Gudrun and Mike, 2020.

CPSIA information can be obtained
at www.ICGtesting.com
Printed in the USA
LVHW061145070221
678629LV00008B/193